AATSP

Professional Development Series
Handbook for Teachers K-16

VOLUME III

The Communicative Classroom

Terry L. Ballman
Judith E. Liskin-Gasparro
Paul B. Mandell

HEINLE & HEINLE
™
THOMSON LEARNING

HEINLE & HEINLE

THOMSON LEARNING

AATSP:
Professional Development Series Handbook for Teachers K-16
Volume III: The Communicative Classroom
Terry L. Ballman, Judith E. Liskin-Gasparro, Paul B. Mandell

President: Dennis Hogan
Publisher: Wendy Nelson
Acquisitions Editor: Helen Richardson
Developmental Editor: Jeff Gilbreath
Marketing Manager: Jill Garrett
Project Manager: Tina Landman
Cover Designer: Candice Swanson
Printer: Quebecor Digital Custom Demand

Printed in the United States of America
1 2 3 4 5 6 7 8 9 10   06 05 04 03 02 01

For more information contact Heinle & Heinle, 25 Thomson Place, Boston, MA 02210 USA,
or you can visit our Internet site at http://www.heinle.com

For permission to use material from this text or product contact us:
Tel   1-800-730-2214
Fax   1-800-730-2215
Web   www.thomsonrights.com

ISBN: 0-03-040779-6

CONTENTS

PREFACE

In this third volume of the AATSP *Professional Development Series Handbook for* Teachers K-16 we start from the premise that most foreign language teachers today want and claim to be teaching for proficiency and to be leading communicative classrooms. Our collective experience of teaching and/or observing in foreign language classrooms at the elementary, middle school, high school, community college, and university levels throughout the U.S. has shown us that the traditional paradigm of teacher-centered grammar instruction is a continuing reality in many language programs. *The Communicative Classroom* is intended to demystify communicative language teaching and to make it accessible to all Spanish teachers. We achieve this, in part, by providing authentic classroom scenarios and numerous suggestions and models of good communicative teaching practices.

In Chapter 1 "The Case for Classroom Communication" we introduce and explain classroom communication in the larger context of communication and the *Standards for Foreign Language Learning in the 21st Century.* We describe our emphasis on the development of speaking as a goal for language learning by both students and teachers through the use of communicative (i.e., task-based) activities. Classroom communication can be a positive, motivating factor for students, and it can also prepare them to use Spanish in the real world beyond the classroom. Several concerns of teachers who do not teach communicatively are discussed, including the belief that teachers must choose between focusing on communication and covering a specified amount of course material.

Chapter 2 "The Role of Grammar in the Communicative Classroom" briefly articulates the two extreme and opposing positions regarding grammar: Grammar has no role in the classroom vs. grammar is the goal of instruction. Our middle-ground position is that grammar should support communication. Within this position we give justification for and numerous examples of explicit grammar instruction, including instruction

i

that is proactive, responsive, and student-initiated. A summary is provided of what teachers should expect regarding grammatical accuracy, the complexity of an activity, and language level.

The organization and design of the communicative classroom is presented in Chapter 3 on "Activity Design and Lesson Planning in the Communicative Classroom. " The chapter begins by comparing sample topics as they might be addressed in a communicative class as opposed to a class focused on grammar. The relationship between the elements in a lesson or unit are explored, as are different activity types (e.g., interviews and information gap activities). We then define task-based instruction and show how it facilitates communicative lesson planning. We also show how learning scenarios suggested by the *Standards* follow activity design and lesson planning that are comparable to task-based instruction.

Some teachers may be hesitant to implement communicative language teaching for fear of how to test their students in a communicative way. Chapter 4 "Evaluation of Oral Communication in the Communicative Classroom" begins by giving some basic information on testing, specifically on the evaluation of speaking. Through the use of concrete examples, the answers to the following questions are provided: What should tests be about? (i.e., What should make up the content of our tests?); how should tests be presented?; and how should tests be scored?

Chapter 5 on "Classroom Interaction" presents numerous examples of authentic interactions—from real-life conversations between adults and small children and between native speakers and non-native speakers—to ESL and foreign language classroom interactions between teachers and students and between one student and another. These interactions are analyzed to highlight preferred classroom practices. What are the best ways, for example, to lead a class discussion? What kinds of questioning behaviors promote better student responses? What types of speaking behaviors should teachers encourage in their students? Does research on the language produced by students working in pairs or small groups on communicative activities support student-centered pedagogical practice? In this chapter we also discuss several teacher beliefs, and how there sometimes is a mismatch between what teachers perceive to be the purpose of an activity and what the outcome of the activity really is.

At the end of each chapter is a section titled "Application Activities for Reflection and Discussion." This section of questions, exercises, and activities is designed to give readers the opportunity not only to think about and discuss the main ideas and suggestions presented in each chapter, but to relate and apply them to their own classrooms.

It is our sincere hope that *The Communicative Classroom* will be a useful tool for both new and experienced teachers of Spanish at all levels of instruction.

ACKNOWLEDGMENTS

We are grateful to **Lynn A. Sandstedt,** past Executive Director of the AATSP, whose idea it was for a book that would serve as a practical guide to communicative language teaching. We thank Lynn for encouraging and supporting us throughout the duration of this project.

We would like to thank our thoughtful, intelligent readers who read and made suggestions from the perspective of the classroom teacher: **Larry P. Fox** (Foreign Language Department Chair at Tuscola High School in Waynesville, NC) and **Brian D. Morrill** (formerly of Los Angeles Unified School District).

We would like to thank **Laura Chapman** (Western Carolina University) for her talented work in turning the manuscript into camera-ready copy. And thanks to Harcourt College Publishers, particularly **Jeff Gilbreath**, **Tina Landman**, and **Phyllis Dobbins**, and to Heinle and Heinle Publishers.

> Terry L. Ballman
> Judith E. Liskin-Gasparro
> Paul B. Mandell

THE CASE FOR CLASSROOM COMMUNICATION

Please choose the most appropriate response.

Question 1: What is classroom communication, and why is it important?
- a. Classroom communication prepares students for real-life communication outside the classroom.
- b. It is motivating.
- c. Carefully constructed communicative activities contribute to language acquisition
- d. All of the statements are correct.

Question 2: If classroom communication is widely recognized as a good thing, why don't teachers do more of it?

- a. We have a fear of inaccuracy.
- b. We believe that accuracy is attainable
- c. Teachers believe that they must choose between communication and coverage.
- d. All of the statements are correct.

INTRODUCTION

When we leaf through a book on foreign language teaching (e.g., Alice Omaggio Hadley's *Teaching Language in Context*), perhaps most striking is the emphasis that our profession has historically placed on the **teaching method** as the key to students' success in learning a language. In fact, learning a second or foreign language[1] comprises a complex and not fully understood interaction of social factors, such as the setting in which the language is learned; existing knowledge and the way

---

[1] The terms "second language (L2)" and "foreign language (FL)" are used interchangeably in this book.

1

the brain processes language; and individual factors, such as age, language aptitude, and motivation (Ellis 1994, p. 193). These factors are themselves complex and interact with each other in numerous ways. For example, the age and educational level at which a person undertakes language study may affect the amount and types of input the person receives (a social factor), as well as how the person processes the input (a processing mechanism issue). It is generally believed that the language learning that takes place in schools is different from the kinds of language learning undertaken by people who live in a country in which the language is spoken, but researchers do not fully understand how the classroom context interacts with the many other factors involved in second language acquisition.

EMPHASIS ON ORAL COMMUNICATION

The purpose of this book is to explore one area of language learning in Spanish classrooms—oral communication. If we go back to our hypothetical foreign language methods course, we can see that no matter what the method or teaching approach, a principal goal of language teaching for several decades has been, and continues to be, speaking proficiency. Even in the beginning of the 20th century, which we often dismiss as the era of the grammar-translation approach, we can see in professional journals that foreign language teachers were debating the same topics that we still discuss today. In the early issues of *The Modern Language Journal*, which began publication in 1916, we can read debates about the theory and practice of language teaching, the balance between attention to meaning and attention to linguistic accuracy, and the place of oral skills in the curriculum (Liskin-Gasparro 2001, pp. 87-88). In more recent times, speaking and communication have been explicitly located at the center of language teaching. The 1980s found us stressing "communicative competence" by focusing on meaning, tasks, and communication (Richards and Rodgers 1986, p. 72). We also worked to integrate proficiency-oriented assessment into all aspects of instructional programs. In the 1990s and continuing in the beginning of the current century, our profession has refined its understanding of and orientation to proficiency and communication by placing greater attention on students' interactions with authentic tasks and authentic materials, made possible by the expansion of multimedia and web technologies.

The central role of oral skills in current-day language instruction has been confirmed in surveys of students and teachers. In a survey of goals for language instruction (Harlow and Muyskens 1994), 1,373 Spanish and French students in intermediate college courses ranked as their highest goal "speaking the language (defined as the ability to communicate in social, travel, and job situations" (p. 145). They also reported in their written comments the importance for them of gaining confidence and being able to speak without fear (p. 145). "Self-confidence" and "speaking" ranked at the top of the goals of the 59 college language instructors in the survey, thus matching the student priorities.

Birckbichler and Corl (1993) conducted a survey of foreign language supervisors at high school and college levels about the extent to which the proficiency movement of the 1980s had influenced and was continuing to influence their choice of classroom activities and teaching methods. The respondents reported that the proficiency movement, particularly the *ACTFL Proficiency Guidelines*, had strongly affected their teaching, and listed partner/small group activities, role plays/simulations, and information gap activities as both most reflective of a proficiency orientation and as among the activity types they most frequently used (p. 27). The paired and small-group activity types listed here are, not surprisingly, most often used to work on speaking skills.

Perhaps it is not necessary to use these surveys to justify writing a book on classroom communication. After all, as readers of these pages are aware and as the foregoing discussion has pointed out, communicative language proficiency has historically occupied a key position in the professional discourse. However, from conversations at conferences and on computer listservs, we also know that drill-based teaching of oral skills has not disappeared and may still figure heavily in the lesson plans of a significant number of language teachers nationwide. One reason for the persistence of traditional, drill-based teaching practices may simply be a lack of information—supported by clear explanations and examples from actual classrooms—about what communicative language teaching is and how it works in practice. With this book we hope to present explanations and examples, anticipate and respond to readers' questions, and assist Spanish teachers in trying out new approaches and activities. Given the rapid rise in the Spanish-speaking population of the U.S., the adult work options of our students are likely to be expanded and enriched if they can speak Spanish well enough to interact with their co-workers at even a simple level. Indeed, many of our students currently work part-time in positions that put them in regular contact with speakers of Spanish. We know from their stories that the quality of their work environment, as well as their access to the world beyond their immediate surroundings, is enhanced by their communicative proficiency in Spanish. But whether our current students spend their adult lives in a predominantly monolingual or, as demographic trends indicate, multilingual work environment, we—their Spanish teachers—may be their best introduction to communication in another language. We want to make that introduction as rich, motivating, and usable as possible.

We begin with a consideration of the two questions posed at the beginning of the chapter: (1) What is classroom communication, and why is it important? and (2) If classroom communication is widely recognized as a good thing, why don't teachers do more of it?

WHAT IS CLASSROOM COMMUNICATION?

DEFINITIONS

To begin with a consideration of the larger concept of **communication** in the context of language instruction in the 21st century, we turn to the *Standards for Foreign Language Learning* (1996). The first standard, Communication, is composed of three modes:

Standard 1.1. Interpersonal: Students engage in conversations, provide and obtain information, express feelings and emotions, and exchange opinions.

Standard 1.2. Interpretive: Students understand and interpret written and spoken language on a variety of topics.

Standard 1.3. Presentational: Students present information, concepts, and ideas to an audience of listeners or readers on a variety of topics.

The broad view of communication proposed in the *Standards* involves all four language skills, not just speaking. In this book, we limit ourselves to **interpersonal speaking**, which constitutes a part of Standard 1.1. However, speaking with another person also involves understanding and interpreting what the other person says (Standard 2.1), and talking about the interaction may involve making a brief presentation (Standard 1.3). In addition, interpersonal communication includes knowledge and skills beyond linguistic proficiency, such as the ability to organize information, formulate an opinion, or make an inference on the basis of partial information or partial comprehension. L2 speakers also need to develop their ability to solve communication problems during an interaction. When they ask the other person to repeat an utterance, to say it more slowly, or to express it in a different way, they are engaging in **negotiation of meaning**. When they don't know how to express in Spanish something they want to say and turn to paraphrases, a simpler way of stating an idea, or even when they make up a word, they are calling on their **communication strategies**. All of

5

their specific linguistic knowledge and their general cognitive skills come into play when they engage in interpersonal communication.

From this broad understanding of communication, we draw our definition of **classroom communication** for this book.

- It is the exchange, interpretation, and expression of meaning (e.g., Savignon 1997). These forms of communication correspond to the interpersonal, interpretive, and presentational standards discussed above.
- Students learn the complex skill of interpersonal communication through communicative activities in class. The best activities are those that have a purpose over and above the pedagogical goal of practicing particular linguistic forms (e.g., using a guide for visitors to Mexico City, decide with a partner on a good schedule of activities for a three-day stay). This type of activity is usually called a **task-based activity**.[2]
- The activities are planned and orchestrated by the teacher, but the students assume responsibility for the exchange, interpretation, and expression of meaning in Spanish.
- Although students are carrying out the activities in the target language and are operating with limited linguistic resources, their attention during the activities is focused primarily on precision of meaning, rather than on accuracy of form.

THE ROLES OF TEACHERS AND STUDENTS IN CLASSROOM COMMUNICATION

Embedded in this definition of classroom communication are some assumptions about the roles of teachers and students. Like teachers of all subjects, Spanish teachers have traditionally

---

[2] Task-based instruction is discussed in detail in Chapter 3.

placed themselves at the center of the classroom action. As the experts in the Spanish language and how to teach it, we believe, and with justification, that our role is to share with our students our knowledge and skill. Given the ratio of 1 teacher for a class of 30 students or more or instructional situations in which the teacher meets with a group of students 1-2 days per week, it is easy to understand why so much of this knowledge sharing takes the form of the teacher explaining, instructing, and demonstrating. In this type of classroom, the students' role is to watch, listen, write down, and understand.

This picture is an exaggeration, of course; active learning-by-doing has also long been a part of the educational landscape. Yet it is sobering to think about how the language of teaching and learning is imbued with the "conduit metaphor" (Reddy 1979), which implies that knowledge can be transmitted from one person to another like a platter of food being passed at the dinner table. We have all participated in conversations with other teachers in which we have heard or said the following:[3]

- "I got this activity from a book on classroom communication I just read."
- "I give away all my good ideas, but nobody else in my department shares any of theirs."
- "My third-period class was not understanding *gustar*, but I finally got through to them."
- "We have a lot of material to pack in before the end of the semester."

When we operate, consciously or unconsciously, within the conduit metaphor we are more likely to spend substantial amounts of class time in direct teaching of vocabulary, cultural information, and particularly, grammatical structures. We imagine that abstract concepts, like grammatical structures, can somehow be transferred into the students' heads and "belong" to students. This is a difficult role to assume, because it places a tremendous burden on the teacher to explain things "the right way" and to "make sure" that students have "understood." This

---

[3] Examples are adapted from Reddy (1979).

role has been referred to as the "Atlas Complex" (Finkel and Monk 1983, p. 85, as cited in Lee and VanPatten 1995, p. 6).

Another way to look at classroom learning—a way more in concert with the notions in this book—is to imagine the teacher as the architect and resource person (Lee and VanPatten 1995, pp. 12-13) in a large, complex building project. The role of the teacher is not to do the actual construction—that is the students' job—but rather to design the meticulous, multifaceted plans that will guide the construction work. In the case of the Spanish classroom, the plans are the activities that comprise the curriculum. The responsibility of the students is to participate fully in the activities. This includes being aware of the goals and objectives that underlie each activity and actively trying to learn as much as possible while engaging in the activities. A day of shoddy construction work can have serious consequences later on. Similarly, doing the activities just to get them done rather than working on them thoughtfully and actively can also have negative consequences for the overall project of FL learning.

Using the building project metaphor, we see that the responsibility for learning lies with the students. Students use all of the resources at their disposal, both internal and external, to create and express meaning. The teacher serves as one of the external resources, clarifying the steps of the activity, answering a vocabulary question, and helping students to stay on task. The teacher's role, then, is very much the role of the expert who designs activities that are engaging, appropriate for the level, and articulated with the rest of the curriculum.

WHY CLASSROOM COMMUNICATION IS IMPORTANT

Classroom communication matters because of its central position in language instruction: Learning to communicate is recognized as a principal goal of language learning and, at the same time, by communicating students learn the language. We expand on this notion in the sections that follow.

PREPARING STUDENTS FOR REAL-LIFE COMMUNICATION

As we discussed above, the respondents in one large-scale survey reported that "speaking the language" was their first goal in studying Spanish or French. What do students mean when they say they want to learn to speak Spanish? Whom do they hope to talk to, and about what? In what contexts? Asking our students these questions may raise their awareness about the possible outcomes of learning Spanish. Thinking about these questions may remind our students that Spanish is more than a school subject. It is a language in which millions of people on a daily basis work, play, watch TV, go out with their friends, and much more. In all of those contexts and the activities associated with them, these millions of people are communicating. Students who learn to "speak Spanish" have access to new friends, new activities, and new places to explore.

If your students are like ours, "speaking Spanish" means, primarily, getting to know other people and learning about new cultures through those personal connections. What do friends talk about, and how do they talk? Among other things, they build a foundation of shared experiences by doing things together, they talk about themselves and about events in the world around them, and they exchange stories. Even though our students already possess in their first language this complex "interpersonal knowledge," their knowledge is tacit, not explicit. They have probably never articulated aloud or may never have thought about how they relate to their friends or what they do to build a friendship with a new acquaintance. It may also not have occurred to them that this knowledge is an internal resource that they can deploy to compensate for their limited proficiency in Spanish.

Students can learn to rely on these and other internal skills in Spanish through classroom communication. We usually think of classroom communication exclusively in the interpersonal mode—talking with another person where both participants have equal roles in the interaction—but learning to tell a good story is also a communicative skill that can be taught in the Spanish class. Following is a story about a skiing accident told by a college student whose speaking proficiency in Spanish is Intermediate High on the ACTFL proficiency scale. Speakers at this level are relatively fluent, although they are not consistently able to talk in the past or find ways to express themselves when they don't know all the vocabulary they need.

The student told this story during an oral proficiency interview (OPI). Asking interviewees to talk about a memorable event is a technique often used in OPIs to elicit a story in past time. Even though this student is a fairly strong speaker, there are several points where he has to overcome a linguistic difficulty to keep his story interesting for the listener. Notice, too, the techniques he uses to introduce drama into his story.

1. estaba esquiando en la montaña
2. y era muy tarde, el último corre del día
3. estaba muy cansado,
4. y mis amigos me dijeron
5. ¡una vez más, una vez más, vamos, vamos!"
6. y me di
7. bueno, vamos"
8. y salté de un . . .
9. no sé,
10. un montón pequeño de nieve *(laugh)*
11. y cuando pone mis pies en la nieve
12. . . no sé cómo se dice .
13. um, mi pie . . . iba en un dirección y mi rodilla en el otro
14. era horrible
15. estaba en un . . . um . . .
16. no sé
17. *cast* . . . casto *(laugh)* por cinco meses
18. tenía que ir a terapia cada día por dos dos meses
19. fue horrible, horrible, una de mis experiencias . . . experimentos malas en mi vida
20. era en el hospital por cinco días con drogas
21. y no puedo dormir
22. y no puedo comer
23. y no puedo hacer nada
24. horrible
25. yo tenía muletas con espigas . . . espigas debajo de las muletas

      para poner en la nieve y hielo
26. yo tenía un hombre
28. que tomeme a mis clases, a la cena, al almuerzo
29. pero no podía hacer muchísimas cosas
           (Liskin-Gasparro 1993, p. 269)

What are the ingredients of this story that make it a good one? Most important, the story has a clear structure. First, the introduction sets the scene for the main event. Second, the accident itself is explained in detail. Finally, the narrator talks about the immediate aftermath in the hospital and the consequences for months afterwards. Interwoven into the basic structure are the details and other narrative strategies that paint a vivid picture for the listener. The opening scene is set with relevant details: It was the end of the day, it was late, and he was tired, but his friends were urging him to take one more run with them. He gives only a little information about the accident, but dwells at length on the aftermath: his drugged state in the hospital, the months of physical therapy, his helplessness.

The two narrative strategies that he uses are reported direct speech (reporting someone's words or thoughts word-for-word as a direct quote) and repetition. These are powerful strategies to highlight and intensify the emotions that he was experiencing, and are used by good storytellers in all languages. In addition, the student narrator uses a good paraphrase for "mogul," a snow bump—he says *un montón pequeño de nieve* (line 10). His invented word—*casto* for "cast" (line 16), is less successful, because a non-English speaker would not have understood it. But all in all, he manages to tell a good story.

Story telling is just one example of an activity that, when treated as classroom communication rather than primarily as practice of linguistic form, prepares students for real-life language use. All of the topics illustrated here—understanding narrative structure, using details to heighten suspense or justify the events of the story, intensifying emotion through reported speech and repetition, and gaining skill and confidence in using compensation strategies like paraphrasing—do involve the forms of the language. However, our point is that it is not necessary for mastery of form to precede attention to these rhetorical issues. Even before students are fully able to handle the linguistic demands of narrative discourse, they can learn to identify intensifiers, react to them in the stories of more expert speakers, and construct collaborative stories. In other words, they can begin very early to implement in Spanish the. narrative devices that make for a good story, devices that they already use unconsciously in their first language.

When students at a lower level of proficiency attempt to tell a story, they need a good deal of structure and support to compensate for the gaps in their linguistic knowledge. In addition, students at the Novice or Intermediate Low or Intermediate Mid levels on the ACTFL scale are often so focused on the linguistic challenge of the task that they forget they can call forth the internal resources for story-telling that they control in their native language. With less-advanced students, a simpler alternative to stories based on personal experience, is to recount a story depicted in a series of drawings. The pictures provide the structure and visual cues that these students need. The Advanced Placement (AP) Program of the College Board uses a picture sequence in its AP Spanish Language Examination, and picture sequences from former years are available to teachers for classroom use. You can see recently used picture sequences on the AP Spanish web page **(http://www.collegeboard.org/ap/students/spanish/frq00/index.html).**

Another approach is to have students engage in simpler forms of extended discourse, such as describing their daily routine or their weekend activities. These are not stories because they deal with routines, rather than specific events, and for that reason require less mental effort. Students are able to concentrate on linguistic accuracy and on connecting sentences together into extended discourse. Here are two samples of college students in a fourth-semester course whose task was to explain to a visitor from Latin America how they spend their weekends. Student 1 produces a lot of language, but notice how incoherent it is. The first two sentences do not hang together and, in fact, almost contradict each other.

> Usualmente durante el fine de semana yo voy
> a las fiestas y me gusta tener un buen tiempo
> toda la fin de semana. Y entonces estudio
> mucho durante la fin de semana porque es
> necesario para recibir un buenas notas porque
> esta escuela es muy difícil. Cuando no va a las
> fiestas me gusta ser un *couch potato* . . . lo
> siento.   (Liskin-Gasparro 1995)

This student is able to communicate a good deal of information. Notice that he limits himself to simple structures, familiar verbs, and phrases that he most likely knows well: *yo voy, estudio, es necesario, buenas notas, me gusta.* He also runs out of steam at the end and does not attempt to express in Spanish what he means by "couch potato." Typical of learners who are pushing themselves beyond their comfort level, he uses two variants of *fin de semana*, both inaccurate: *el fine de semana* and *la fin de semana.* Teachers often wonder why students cannot control simple vocabulary and structures that they have learned and practiced extensively, like *el fin de semana* or *yo voy.* Our explanation is that creating and sustaining meaning over several sentences requires so much mental and linguistic energy that learners do not have enough left over to monitor the language that they produce. With time and practice in speaking in extended discourse, some of the processes become automatic, which allows students to devote more attention to the other processes.

We also see considerable variation in how students choose to deal with the competing demands of making meaning and attending to linguistic accuracy. Student 2 relies more heavily than Student 1 on phrases like *muchas veces* and *a veces* to organize her discourse.

> Usualmente estudio para mis clases o voy a
> fiestas con mis amigos. Muchas veces llamo
> mis amigos que vivir en otros estados o
> escribo cartas para mis amigos. A veces
> limpio mis ropa que es sucio y a veces limpio

mi alcoba y en los fines de semanas me gusta
dormó . . . duermo muy muy tarde.
(Liskin-Gasparro 1995)

We can teach students to consciously employ the strategies
that these students have used. Both students use adverbial
phrases (e.g., *a veces, usualmente, entonces*) to link sentences
together logically. We can also show students that using short
sentences with a similar structure will enable them to produce a
lot of language without a great deal of mental energy. We can
use other (anonymous, preferably from previous years) students'
descriptions of their weekend activities as grammar lessons and
as lessons in how to maximize meaning and maintain
comprehensibility. In the examples above, we see that the
students invariably make errors when they attempt complex
sentences (e.g., *llamo mis amigos que vivir en otros estados*), but
are able to achieve more accuracy when they keep it simple.
These practical strategies will help students produce more
meaningful speech earlier in their study of Spanish.

CLASSROOM COMMUNICATION IS MOTIVATING

Language teachers often talk about student motivation as though
it were a stable characteristic that students bring with them into
the language classroom, like their eye color or ethnicity. Early
motivation theories, particularly that of Gardner and Lambert
(1972), stressed the importance of the attitude of the language
learner to the culture and to speakers of the second language.
According to Lambert (1974, p. 98), an integrative orientation
involves "a sincere and personal interest in the people and
culture represented by the other language group," whereas an
instrumental orientation was associated with an interest in "the
practical value and advantages of learning a new language."
Developed in Canada, the Gardner and Lambert model
emphasized the social context of language learning, not the
classroom context (Dörnyei 1994, p. 273). Not until the 1990s
were theories of motivation developed based on research with
classroom learners. Newer models of motivation are far more

complex than their antecedents, taking into account the multiple levels of influence, both internal and external, on second language learners.

Common sense also tells us that classroom communication—communicative, task-based activities as an integral part of the curriculum—may contribute positively to students' motivation to study the language. Dörnyei's (1994) framework of foreign language learning motivation has three levels: the language level (i.e., general perceptions about the language and the culture), the learner level (e.g., self-confidence, anxiety about speaking in front of other people), and the learning situation level (e.g., interest in the course, group cohesion, teacher's approach to learning activities).

The connections between Dörnyei's framework and classroom communication are immediately seen at the level of the learning situation. If students find the course interesting and relevant to their needs and if they experience success and satisfaction in that success, they are motivated to participate and to persist. Similarly, if the teacher fosters that interest and perception of relevance by assuming a collaborative (rather than authoritative) stance and fosters success by presenting and modeling tasks well and giving ample feedback, then students again are motivated to participate fully and to continue language study. Finally, if working with the group is rewarding—if students support each other, are given opportunities for autonomy in the selection of activities, and are rewarded for successful collaborations—then this, too, contributes to increased overall satisfaction with the course and enhances motivation.

Classroom communication as defined earlier in this chapter has many of the elements that are believed to promote motivation and contribute to productive L2 learning. Perhaps most obvious, and yet most important, students who regularly engage in carefully constructed task-based activities learn how to listen, to trust their ability to extrapolate and form hypotheses, and to use what they know in novel and creative ways. In other words, they learn to do what they practice doing. Task-based activities by their very nature take the expert (the teacher) out of the picture, thus setting the stage for the students to push themselves to the next level, whatever that "next level" may be. For students whose goal is to learn to speak the language, building their confidence and experience though classroom communication is bound to bring satisfaction and the desire to learn more.

How can a teacher promote students' expectation that they will make progress in learning Spanish? How can they build motivation to learn Spanish into the classroom culture? One way is to explain to students that all of their classroom activities, even those that are "fun," have a purpose related to learning, and to make sure that students understand the goals of each activity. Then, teachers should establish a repertoire of activity types that students come to recognize. Once this happens, it is not necessary to go through lengthy explanations and directions for each activity, because students know already how the activity will proceed. A second technique is to follow a careful sequence of steps in setting up an activity. These "Tips for Managing Pair and Small-Group Activities," presented in Figure 1 (Liskin-Gasparro 1999), are general enough to apply to all kinds of activities.

Figure 1. Tips for managing pair and small-group activities

1. Design activities that are short, with specific outcomes. Until students are used to these activities, avoid complex ones with several stages. (Students will get off-task.) Remind students of the purpose of the activity.
2. Make directions clear and simple. Deliver directions in several ways:
   - Say them orally.
   - Write a brief version on the board for student reference.
   - Write them on activity sheets (handouts) if you use one.
   - Give a model. If possible, write a model on the handout if possible.
3. Circulate during the activity.

- Provide needed vocabulary and key pieces of grammatical information as needed.
- Keep students on task.
- Stay alert to detect students talking in English, not following instructions, etc.

4. Discourage writing, since these are oral activities. Limit writing to short notes or filling out forms.

5. End the activity a little bit too soon.
   - This discourages the use of English.
   - It is better for some not to finish than for others to finish and start chatting in English.

6. Always include in the activity a follow-up or feedback phase.
   - Purpose: for students to share the information they have gotten during the activity.
   - Make sure that the gathering of information has been meaningful and purposeful.
   - Design this follow-up phase so that students are required to listen to each other and, if possible, do something with the information that other students provide.
   - Student reports during this follow-up phase should be oral (speaking), not reading from a written text.
   - Develop a repertoire of follow-up activities.

7. Include a short reminder of the linguistic purpose of the activity: "Why did we just do this? What language forms did we practice?"

8. Any grammar instruction based on errors that emerge during activities of this type should take place after the activity is over, and should focus only on 1-2 errors that are common to the group.

(Liskin-Gasparro 1999)

Task-based activities promote group cohesiveness because invariably the performance of the pair or the group depends on collaboration and mutual support among the members. Teachers can emphasize the importance of collaboration by building it into their evaluation system. (See Chapter 4, "Evaluation of Oral

Communication in the Communicative Classroom.") Many students respond enthusiastically to games and competition, so activities in which groups of students vie to construct "the most elaborate plan" or "the most useful list of suggestions" are often quite successful.

CAREFULLY CONSTRUCTED ACTIVITIES CONTRIBUTE TO LANGUAGE ACQUISITION

Researchers in second language acquisition (SLA) have proposed several theoretical models of interest to language teachers. Perhaps the best known SLA theorist is Stephen Krashen (1982, 1985), whose Input Hypothesis claimed that simply being exposed to comprehensible input (assuming a positive affective environment) was sufficient for language acquisition to take place. For Krashen, the processes of acquisition—moving from comprehension of content to making the connections between form and meaning at an abstract level—proceed unconsciously, making unnecessary or even useless such traditional activities as explaining structures, engaging in speaking activities, or error correction by the teacher.

Although Krashen's theory has been heavily criticized by other SLA researchers as unsupported and untestable, the controversy surrounding it may have contributed to increased interest in SLA theory. Two SLA theories of the 1980s in which classroom communication occupies an important place are Swain's (1985) Comprehensible Output Hypothesis and Long's (1983) Interaction Hypothesis. A Canadian researcher interested in immersion education, Swain had studied the developing proficiency of Anglophone students whose entire elementary and secondary education took place in the L2 (French). In other words, students graduating from high school had experienced 12 years of comprehensible input, as well as some L2 instruction (in language arts classes). Although the students' comprehension was native-like, their spoken French was fluent but filled with grammatical and lexical errors. Swain concluded that students were able to achieve native-like levels of comprehension by understanding the meaning and by guessing meaning from the context, and did not need to process the grammatical forms of the input to do so. In contrast, when speaking or writing, students were forced to notice the gap between what they wanted to express and the linguistic means at their disposal. Swain hypothesized that awareness of the gap and their need to make meaning impelled learners to form new hypotheses about the language and to try them out. This process, she believes, facilitates the processes that are the substance of language acquisition.

Whereas Swain's Comprehensible Output Hypothesis focuses on the learner's internal, mental struggle to make meaning with limited resources, Long's Interaction Hypothesis relies on the collaboration of a conversation partner to trigger and facilitate these same processes. When students are working to understand and make themselves understood to others, their attention is drawn to the details of the language that make the communication happen. When a student has to negotiate meaning (talk back and forth to figure out how to say something or what something means), the process leads to the formation of meaning-form connections and the creation of new knowledge. Two examples will illustrate how this process may work.

The following example (Bearden 2000) comes from an interaction between a student in a second-year college Spanish class and a native speaker (NS) of Spanish from Mexico. Communicating in a computer chat environment, their task was to discover through conversation whether the drawings they had were the same or different. The interaction is reproduced exactly as it appeared in the transcript of the chat session. (The chat program does not accept written accent marks.)

1. NS: tienes tu **hoja**?
2. Student: que es **hoja**?
            en ingles
3. NS: las imagenes
4. Student: si

		Yo tengo **una hoja** de la gente en la playa, jugando volibol
5.	NS:	cual crees que sean iguales?
6.	Student:	si
		tu tienes **ese hoja**?
7.	NS:	es la figura 4?
8.	Student:	si
9.	NS:	OK entonces si la tengo

(Bearden 2000)

In this interaction, the student does not recognize the word *hoja* and asks for a translation. The native speaker instead offers a synonym (*imágenes*), which the student accepts. Notice that twice after that (lines 4, 6) the student uses the word. The negotiation of meaning about that word brought it to her conscious attention so that it became part of her active vocabulary.

The second example (taken from Gass and Varonis 1994) also shows how meaning may be negotiated in an interaction between a nonnative speaker (NNS) and a native speaker (NS), in this case of English. The experiment, which consisted of a game in which one person had to direct the other to place figures in particular locations on a landscape scene, was conducted in two phases. In the first phase, the NS gave instructions to the NNS, and in the second phase the NNS gave instructions to the NS. In both phases, half of the NNS participants were permitted to negotiate for meaning and the other half were not. The researchers found that the NNSs who were permitted to negotiate for meaning in the first phase were more successful at giving directions in the second phase. This was not because they had learned new vocabulary items in the first phase, but rather because they had internalized the descriptive devices that the NSs had used in the first phase.

First phase

Jane: All right, now, above the sun place the squirrel. He's right on top of the sun.

Hiroshi: What is . . . the word?

Jane: OK. The sun.

Hiroshi: Yeah, sun, but . . .

Jane: Do you know what the sun is?

Hiroshi: Yeah, of course. Wh-what's the

Jane: Squirrel. Do you know what a squirrel is?

Hiroshi: No.

Second phase

Hiroshi: The second thing will be . . . put here. This place is . . . small animal which **eats nuts**.

Jane: Oh, squirrel?

Hiroshi: Yeah (*laughter*).

                   (Gass and Varonis 1994, p. 296)

This brief foray into SLA research and theory shows us that meaningful, communicative, collaborative talk in the Spanish classroom creates the conditions for language acquisition to take place. In exchanging information with other students, or in working together to prepare a report or a story for the class, students are negotiating meaning, discovering and constructing form-meaning connections, and creating new knowledge. Some researchers (e.g., Donato 1994) have shown that collaborative work by students without the participation of the teacher or another expert (e.g., the NS in the Gass and Varonis study) still provides opportunities for members of the group to synthesize, clarify, and expand their knowledge of grammar and vocabulary.

Activities or games in which two people have the complementary information needed to solve a puzzle or complete a task are called "information gap activities." In the first example above, the two participants had to figure out if their pictures were the same or different. In the second example, both participants had a landscape scene. One participant had a complete scene, while the other had only the background, along with a stack of items (tree, plant, flower, animals, etc.) that had to be placed in precise locations on the landscape according to directions from the first participant. Another version of the activity in the first example is two drawings that differ in several small details. Without looking at each other's drawings, the two participants have to discover the differences through detailed descriptions of their own drawings. The goal of this type of activity is not the completion of the activity per se, but the interaction that is necessary to carry it out. According to both Long's Interaction Hypothesis and Swain's Output Hypothesis, the need to communicate precisely and accurately pushes learners to attend closely to the connection between their intended meaning and the linguistic means to express that meaning that the language provides. This close attention to form-meaning connections is believed to advance the process of language acquisition.

In the next section we turn to some myths about classroom communication that may stand in the way of teachers deciding to incorporate it in their own programs.

WHY MANY TEACHERS DO NOT TEACH COMMUNICATIVELY

There may be many reasons why teachers do not teach communicatively. In this section we describe the three reasons we find to be most prevalent: (a) we avoid classroom communication because we have a fear of inaccuracy, (b) we avoid classroom communication because we believe that accuracy is attainable, and (c) we believe that we must choose between communication and coverage.

TEACHERS FEAR INACCURACY

Those of us who participated in language instruction in the era of audiolingualism (ALM) as either teachers or students remember well the tightly scripted lessons that were its hallmark. Student activities consisted largely of imitating spoken models (the teacher or an audio tape) and completing pattern drills. Teachers were trained to permit students to say only what they had previous listened to, and to write only those forms they had read. One reason for controlling teacher input and student output to such a degree was to avoid error. If a language is learned by imitation of native or native-like models and repetition of phrasal patterns, the reasoning went, students who hear errors will imitate them and will be doomed to learn error-laden language. If students can be prevented from hearing or making errors, then the language acquisition process can be speeded up, progress more smoothly, and have a more favorable outcome. Consequently, every attempt was made to keep students from making errors in the first place by limiting oral production to closely controlled pattern practice. When students did make errors, they were corrected immediately and explicitly.

Although the principles on which this belief was based have long since been discredited (see discussion in the following section), the fear of inaccuracy is still with us. As recently as 1991, a prominent figure in the foreign language field wrote in alarm in an editorial in *The Modern Language Journal* about communicative classrooms in which were found "large quantities of comprehensible input in the form of highly motivating but highly inaccurate peer speech . . . As students hear themselves and their classmates producing all sorts of creative language, replete with errors, they begin to acquire and internalize these inaccurate forms" (Valette 1991, p. 327). Although Valette's position provoked an immediate and articulate response on theoretical grounds in the next issue of the journal, it is safe to say that many teachers have similar fears—that errors are contagious, spreading from one student to the rest of the class; and that errors left uncorrected will become permanent fixtures in students' language system.

The fact is that generations of grammar-centered instruction, coupled with extensive attention to error avoidance and correction by students and teachers, have not succeeded in avoiding error. In addition, research does not support the fear that learners who interact with each other in communicative activities are more likely to produce more errors than when they talk to native speakers (Lightbown and Spada 1993, p. 115). As mentioned above, studies of interactions during pair and group work suggest that students do learn from each other. Thus, the fear that students working in groups are more prone to internalize inaccuracy appears to be groundless.

TEACHERS BELIEVE ACCURACY IS ATTAINABLE

How many times have we said to ourselves: "If only I could spend more time on _____ (complete with the grammar point of your choice), I am sure the students would finally get it"? This is the "impossible dream" of language teachers who have not investigated in their own classroom the connection (or lack of it) between what they teach and how students incorporate the information into their developing language systems. The knowledge that students use in their own speech constitutes what is "learnable" for them. This is the knowledge that they are able to internalize and use in constructing their developing L2 systems.

The awareness that error is unavoidable and a natural part of the process of learning a second language was first explained by Corder (1967). He proposed that the systematic nature of students' errors was significant, because it revealed the state of the student's language system, what he called "transitional competence." A student's errors were valuable to the teacher for the information they gave about the state of the student's developing grammatical system, and valuable to the student as a trigger for testing hypotheses about the grammar of the L2. Corder was also one of the first SLA researchers to point out that learners' errors resulted from not only interference from the native language, but also from universal processes of acquisition; that is, processes that all learners of any FL will pass through.

We can see in our students' errors evidence of processes of transfer from English (e.g., *yo me gusta*) but also processes of overgeneralization (e.g., *diez y cinco*). We also know that when students learn a new structure, they tend to overuse it (e.g., after learning about reflexive verbs, they make all verbs reflexive). Developmental sequences in the acquisition of some structures have been identified, such as question formation in English or past tenses in Spanish. Learners go through the stages in the same order, regardless of their first language. These are all indications that errors are a natural and necessary part of acquisition, and that error-free learner language is simply not attainable.

TEACHERS BELIEVE THEY MUST CHOOSE BETWEEN COMMUNICATION AND COVERAGE

As language teachers, we are aware that students in our courses are subjected to far more linguistic information than they can absorb and use. College programs are obsessed with coverage: Virtually all first-year college Spanish books cover the full range of grammatical structures, including preterite and imperfect, present and imperfect subjunctive, and the major uses of *ser* vs. *estar* and *por* vs. *para*, just to name a few. Although we may reduce the grammar load by eliminating sections and sometimes entire chapters, we are still faced with far more material than can realistically fit into a year of instruction.

However, even if we could reduce the linguistic content of our courses to a reasonable level, we would still need to make the crucial decisions about how to approach the material, what aspects to highlight, and how to integrate each topic into the whole. Our position is that communication need never be sacrificed to coverage, but advocate instead that it be considered an integral part of coverage. As we have discussed in the foregoing sections, classroom communication is a vehicle for acquisition. Covering grammatical structures without giving students ample opportunity to work with them productively and autonomously can, at best, only familiarize students with them. One great benefit of classroom instruction is that it affords the learner opportunities to make form-meaning connections in an environment where linguistic stimuli are controlled in ways that are not possible outside the classroom. It is, as work by Swain (1985) and Long (1985) has shown, through classroom communication that these form-meaning connections are made.

SUMMARY

This chapter has introduced and explained classroom communication in the larger context of communication and the *Standards for Foreign Language Learning in the 21st Century*. The primacy of speaking as a goal for language learning by both students and teachers was also explored. Then, in our discussion of classroom communication, we showed how communicative, task-based activities contribute to language acquisition. We concluded with a brief discussion to allay fears of rampant inaccuracy and inadequate coverage of material.

The chapters that follow expand on the topics that have been raised here. The next chapter, "The Role of Grammar in the Communicative Classroom," treats in detail the integration of grammar into the goal of building students' communicative competence through task-based activities.

APPLICATION ACTIVITIES FOR REFLECTION AND DISCUSSION

1. Become more aware of the presence of the conduit metaphor in our everyday talk about communication. Join a conversation (with other teachers, or with a group of your friends), and listen carefully for instances of the conduit metaphor. [Examples: "I am going to give her a call tonight"; "I took his comments to heart and plan to make some changes."] Write them down as you hear them, and then reflect on the how the conduit metaphor may affect our ideas about teaching and learning. What is the role of the listener who "gets" a call or "takes" comments in the interaction? Is meaning like a package that can be conveyed "unopened" from one person to another?

2. What are your students' reasons for studying Spanish? Create and analyze a survey for your students by following these steps:
   a. Through individual reflection and brainstorming with others, create a preliminary list of questions.
   b. Find the article by Harlow and Muyskens (*Modern Language Journal*, 1994) about their survey of intermediate college Spanish and French students, and adapt questions from their survey instrument that you want to use.
   c. Create your survey instrument. Ask a friend or two to try it out for you, and to point out ambiguities, repetitions, or other problems. Make the necessary revisions.
   d. Administer the questionnaire to your students, or to all Spanish or all foreign language students in your school.
   e. Tabulate and analyze your results. What do they tell you about students' reasons for studying Spanish? What new information have you discovered? How might you apply that information to your teaching?

3. In this chapter we analyzed the techniques used by a narrator when telling a story in Spanish: story structure (setting the scene, the climax, the aftermath), use of repetition and reported speech as intensifiers, and paraphrasing and word coinage to smooth over gaps in vocabulary. What strategies can you find in this story? Would you consider this a good story if a friend told it during a conversation? Why or why not? The speaker is a college student whose proficiency is at the Advanced level in Spanish. The story is about a confrontation she had with an angry customer when she worked in a restaurant.

1. bueno es un restaurante muy popular
2. y no se acepta reservaciones
3. y la gente tienen que llevar chaquetas
4. y llegan los clientes
5. apunto el nombre, el apellido y la hora
6. y digo
7. "bueno, tardamos una hora
8. tardamos una hora y media"
9. y siempre después de veinte minutos, quince minutos me acercan
10. y me preguntan
11. "bueno es que estoy aquí desde hace hora y media"
12. y decía
13. "lo siento, señor
14. pero hace diez minutos que estás, que está usted aquí, etc."
15. y una vez era horrible
16. la, es un restaurante familiar
17. quiero decir
18. que hay un dueño . . .una mujer dueña y sus hijos
19. y ella tiene muchas reglas en cuanto al comportamiento de los clientes y especialmente en cuanto a la ropa
20. si se quita la chaqueta una persona,
21. tenemos que avisarlo
22. tienes que llevar la chaqueta en el comedor

23. lo siento"
24. y una vez me acer . . . vi a una persona sin chaqueta
25. y le avisé
26. "lo siento
27. pero tienes que poner la chaqueta"
28. y se enfadó como un animal
29. y me llamó por teléfono después de salir
30. con un promeso de que alguien va a pegarme en la cabeza
31. era horrible
32. era horrible

(Liskin-Gasparro 1993, p. 312)

4. Select an activity from your textbook that is done in pairs or small groups. Using the "Tips for managing pair and small-group activities" (pp. 16-17), create a detailed lesson plan for the activity. First, decide on the purposes for your activity: What is your communicative goal? What tasks will students carry out? What is the linguistic purpose of the activity? Then create your lesson plan. Include the script for the directions you will give orally, a handout (or transparency for students to use as a guide) for students to record the information they get from their partners, and your plan for the follow-up phase.

5. Investigate how your students collaborate in producing a narrative based on a sequence of pictures. [If you have advanced students who have experience in talking in the past, ask them to narrate the story using preterite and imperfect verb forms. Otherwise, they can create their story in the present tense.] Put students in pairs of about equal proficiency in Spanish (to encourage equal participation), and have them write the story suggested by the sequence of pictures. As they work, they should talk to each other (in either English or Spanish) to make their story as linguistically accurate as possible. Record their conversation on audio or video. Afterwards, transcribe the tape, and analyze it to get a better picture of students' understanding of grammatical

rules, their guessing strategies, etc. Can you find evidence that two students who collaborate in a task like this are providing the context for each student to learn?

THE ROLE OF GRAMMAR IN THE
COMMUNICATIVE CLASSROOM

Please choose the most appropriate response.

Question 1. What "middle of the road" role should grammar
play in the communicative classroom?
 a. Grammar has no explicit role in the classroom.
 b. Grammatical knowledge and mastery is the goal
 of language learning.
 c. Grammar should be taught insofar as it supports
 communicative goals.

Question 2: How is this position manifested in the Spanish
classroom?
 a. Students will learn Spanish grammar through
 rich exposure to the language in a variety of
 contexts. It is not necessary, then, to teach
 grammar.
 b. Spanish grammar is taught and practiced so that
 students gain mastery over the linguistic
 system.
 c. Grammatical goals are embedded in
 communicative activities, and the teacher seizes
 opportunities for relevant grammatical
 instruction.

INTRODUCTION

Our experiences as Spanish teachers, teacher trainers, and
classroom observers at both the secondary and post-secondary
levels suggest that a teacher's beliefs about the role of grammar
instruction--be these beliefs conscious or not—directly correlate

with what and how he or she teaches. Those who believe that grammar has no explicit role in the classroom may focus their instruction on the teaching of vocabulary, with emphasis on speaking. Those who believe that the knowledge and mastery of grammar is the learning objective may conduct a teacher-centered class in which grammar drills and practice are commonplace.

For our purposes, we broadly define grammar as the teaching of verb morphology (e.g., preterite forms) and the rules of usage of a given grammatical structure (e.g., word order of direct object pronouns). In this chapter we present two opposing perspectives on the role of grammar in language teaching, and then make the case for grammar in support of communication. Although this is not a book on the teaching of grammar, we explain our middle-ground position. Preceding our position are brief summaries of the two extreme views on the role of grammar in the language classroom, illustrated in Figure 1. We acknowledge that most language teachers' views fall someplace between the two extremes, and that the majority of these are closer to the "Grammar for grammar's sake" than to the "No grammar instruction" position.

Figure 1. Continuum of views on the role of grammar instruction

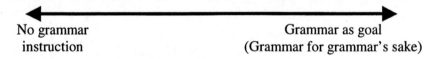

No grammar   Grammar as goal
instruction   (Grammar for grammar's sake)

GRAMMAR HAS NO ROLE IN THE CLASSROOM

At one extreme is the perception that grammar instruction has no purpose in the classroom. This view is derived from the belief that grammar instruction does not have an effect on language development. Those in support of this view (see, for example, Krashen 1982 and 1985; Krashen and Terrell 1983; Schwartz 1993) maintain that only through exposure to comprehensible input will language acquisition occur; and that students will naturally acquire knowledge about the linguistic system through the comprehension of language.

Others who hold the view that grammar has no role in the classroom may consider themselves to be communicative language teachers, and may thus (mis)interpret the term "communicative" as referring to an emphasis on conversational activities, with no attention paid to language structure. This belief assumes that language teaching and learning consists of nothing more than role playing, skits, vocabulary games, and conversation activities, that is, the "fun and games" classroom. In short, this view presumes that as long as one's message is understood or conveyed, success is attained regardless of grammatical accuracy. The rendering of a sentence such as *Juan es hablar español* would be considered acceptable Spanish if it is a logical utterance (i.e., in response to the question, *¿Qué está haciendo Juan?*)

GRAMMAR FOR GRAMMAR'S SAKE

At the other extreme is the perception that a language is fully described by its structure and vocabulary; and if this is the case, then teaching should focus on those two areas. A teacher who advocates this position may say: "You don't really know a language until you've mastered its grammar." Such a teacher is also likely to say: "It's my responsibility to teach my students as much as possible about English grammar." A teacher with this viewpoint is likely to design instruction around grammatical goals: "Today we're going to learn the conditional," "This week we're going to learn the differences between the preterite and the imperfect."

Commonplace to this classroom are drills, in which students practice a targeted grammatical feature. Several examples of drills are provided below:

Example A. The teacher (T) calls out subject pronouns, the class (C) conjugates a target verb to match each subject pronoun.

T: El verbo *hablar*...Nosotros...

C: hablamos.

T: Ella…

C: habla.

Example B. Students are given a passage with present tense verbs. Students are asked to change verbs into the preterite.

Example C. After explaining the rules and formation of direct object pronouns, the teacher asks students to answer his questions using a direct object pronoun.

T: John, ¿conoces a Laura?

J: Sí, la conozco.

T: Bien. Laura, ¿conoces a Jennifer?

In none of these examples is the focus on meaning. In other words, the goals of the above-mentioned exercises are to practice the targeted grammatical features. In Examples A and B, it is possible to successfully do the exercises and yet have no understanding of their meaning. Example C suggests that some attention be paid to meaning, but most of the focus is on the practice of correct direct object pronominal forms and word order.

Teachers who believe in the "grammar for grammar's sake" position are likely to have grammatical accuracy as a goal. This position views all errors as wrong and in need of correction. Errors are viewed as negative, as they lead to bad habits. Teachers with this belief take on a role of "grammar police" because they feel that it is their responsibility as professionals to correct errors, and that to not correct them would be unprofessional. To help ensure that fewer student errors are produced, these teachers limit classroom activities to those of grammar drill and practice.

GRAMMAR IN SUPPORT OF COMMUNICATION

As shown in Figure 2, the "middle-ground" view—where we position ourselves—proposes that grammar has value insofar as it supports communication. In other words, explicit grammar instruction has a definite role in the classroom, but it is not the goal of instruction. Other arguments in support of explicit grammar instruction are that secondary and college students have generally passed the point where they can just "pick up" grammar from the input, particularly features not salient to them. One example is present subjunctive morphology (in all but *nosotros* and *vosotros* forms), in that the mood is marked in unstressed syllables: *Quiero que me hables, Dudo que coma bien.* From an affective standpoint it is noteworthy that students after a certain age expect explicit grammar instruction because they perceive it to be helpful and necessary. To not teach them grammar may cause them to feel that they are being shortchanged.

Figure 2. Continuum of views on the role of grammar instruction

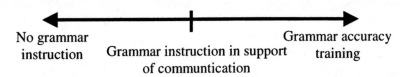

No grammar instruction

Grammar instruction in support of communtication

Grammar accuracy training

Within this position, the question is not *if* grammar should be taught, but rather *what* grammar should be taught, and *how* it should be taught (VanPatten 1988). In our view, the amount, timing, and method of presentation are crucial, and differ greatly from the "grammar for grammar's sake" position. The question of what grammar to teach is predicated on communicative goals; in other words, on what we want students to be able to do. On a lesson on *la casa*, for example, a communicative goal may be: Working in pairs, students will describe a picture of a house to a partner, who will draw it. This communicative goal would determine what language (vocabulary and grammar) students would need in order to achieve the goal. In addition to the vocabulary of parts of the house and furnishings, students would need to use *hay, estar* + location—specifically *está and están*— in order to describe the existence and location of the house's rooms and furnishings. And the success of the activity would be determined by the product; namely, did students draw an accurate rendering of the house?

In order to successfully achieve the communicative goal of drawing the house, students do not have to know that *hay* is from the infinitive *haber*. They do not have to know all the differences in usage between *ser* and *estar*. They do not have to know all the forms of *estar*. Of course the teacher could decide to share this extra linguistic information with students, but he or she should not view it as essential to the stated communicative goal.

For a lesson on nutrition, students could be given the communicative goal of making recommendations based on a classmate's reported eating habits. Assuming that students had learned vocabulary concerning foods, drinks and had familiarity with recommended daily nutritional guidelines, what grammar would students need to know? In order to interview and find out the eating habits of a classmate, students would need to use second person singular preterite forms, for example: *¿Qué desayunaste? ¿Qué comiste por la tarde? ¿Cuántos vasos de agua bebiste ayer?* And later, in order to make their recommendations on a classmate's nutritional habits, students would need to be familiar with the third-person singular present subjunctive verb forms, and how these forms are used:

Recomiendo que mi compañera beba más agua.
Es importante que coma menos dulces, y más vegetales.

In order to successfully achieve the communicative goal of making recommendations regarding a classmate's eating habits, students do not have to know all the contexts in which the subjunctive mood is used. They do not have to use all present subjunctive verb morphology, nor do they have to know that there are matrix and embedded clauses, null subjects, and a pleonastic pronominal in these sentences. Again the teacher could decide to share this linguistic information with students, but the teacher should not view it as necessary for achieving the communicative goal.

EXPLICIT GRAMMAR INSTRUCTION

Although we argue that grammar teaching is necessary for secondary and college-level (adult) students, the typical student has limited grammar knowledge in the first language (L1). And as it is difficult for students to relate new grammatical knowledge in second language (L2) to their L1, long, technical explanations are not helpful. In addition, such explanations are often done in English, which contributes to a student belief that English is for the "serious stuff" (grammar) while Spanish is reserved for the "fluff" (communicative activities). This is hardly the impression we want to make. Grammar instruction should be thought of as providing the tools that students need for communication, and explanations should be designed accordingly.

Below you will find several examples of communicative goals, each accompanied by three types of grammatical information: "essential," "extra" and "non-essential." By "essential" we of course mean information that should be presented to students. It is simple, to-the-point, and helps students achieve the stated communicative goal. "Extra" refers to grammatical information a teacher may wish to share with students. Although having this information does not necessarily help students carry out the communicative task, it may help them see the "big picture." And by "non-essential" we mean grammatical information that is superfluous to students' ability to achieve the communicative goal, and that may actually confuse students. This type of information is likely to distract students from the communicative goal at hand.

A note is in order here regarding the relationship between grammar explanations and language level. The lower the language level, the simpler the grammatical explanation should be. Do first year Spanish students, for example, need to know all the uses of *por* and *para*, when—depending on the communicative goal—knowing one or two uses may suffice? Do beginning level students of Spanish need to know anything at all about the imperfect subjunctive? Yet in contrast with beginning

37

students, advanced level students of Spanish do indeed need to be familiar with all the uses of *por* and *para*, and with the imperfect subjunctive. This is not to say that advanced level students have "mastered" these grammatical features of Spanish, nor that they are not in need of additional or "recycled" grammatical instruction. In fact, the higher the language level, the more grammatical detail a student can be provided.

Communicative goal A: Individual students are asked to identify several of their favorite leisure activities.
Essential grammar explanation:
In order to talk about what I do, the verb almost always ends in –*o*. Examples: *Leo una novela, nado, hago ejercicio.* One exception is *voy*, which comes from the verb *ir > voy al parque.*
Extra grammatical information:
This is called the present indicative tense and these forms refer to the first-person singular.
Non-essential grammatical information:
-There are three declensions: *-ar, -er,* and *–ir* verbs
-The forms for the subject pronouns *tú, él, ella, Ud., nosotros, vosotros, ellos, ellas, Uds.* in the present indicative are....
-Several irregular verbs are *ser > soy, estar > estoy,* etc. Some verbs are irregular in the first-person singular form, like *tener > tengo.* (Note: This information is non-essential in that students will **not** need to use *soy, estoy, tengo* when talking about their favorite leisure activities.)

Communicative goal B: Interview a partner about what he or she did last weekend.
Essential grammar explanation:
In order to ask a classmate: questions about what he or she did recently, most verbs end in –*aste* or –*iste.* Some examples are: *¿Almorzaste en un restaurante?, ¿Fuiste al cine?, ¿Trabajaste?*
Extra grammatical information:
When talking about activities you did in the past, you use what is called the preterite.

Non-essential grammatical information:
-The preterite is one of the two major past tenses in Spanish. The other is called the imperfect.
-The differences between the preterite and the imperfect are....
-The forms for the other subject pronouns in the preterite are....

Communicative goal C: Students are asked to share their opinions of several of their favorite and least favorite subject areas.
Essential grammar explanation:
To be able to express whether or not you like a subject area, you can use the constructions *Me gusta(n)* or *No me gusta(n)*.
You use *gusta* with singular subject areas (e.g., la historia), and *gustan* with plural subject areas (e.g., las matemáticas.) Examples are: *Me gusta el español, Me gustan las ciencias, No me gusta el inglés.*
Extra grammatical information:
English has no exact equivalent for Spanish *gustar* constructions. While in English we say *I like*, in Spanish we say that something is pleasing or not pleasing to me. The rendering in English for *Me gustan las ciencias*, for example, would literally be *Sciences are pleasing to me.* As you can see from this example, *ciencias* is the subject of the sentence.
Non-essential grammatical information:
-*Me* is an indirect object pronoun. Indirect object pronouns refer to a person to whom or for whom something is done.
-The indirect object pronouns for the other persons are: *te, le,* etc.
-Other reverse-construction verbs like *gustar* are *encantar, faltar, importar, interesar,* etc.

The above-mentioned examples are intended to illustrate that grammar explanations should be relevant to communicative goals. Essential grammar explanation helps the student carry out the communicative function, and "too much information" only burdens the student by distracting him or her from the communicative goal. Decisions regarding what explicit grammar information to present depend on the complexity of the communicative goal, and the language level of the students. The more complex the communicative goal and the higher the student language level, the more thorough the grammatical explanation needs to be. Teachers should not assume that because students have studied a particular grammatical feature they have "mastered" it. Students benefit from reminders and revisits with previously studied grammatical features.

INPUT ACTIVITIES

Have you ever noticed that most textbooks present a particular grammatical feature, and then in the first exercise or activity require students to produce it? Would it not be wiser to provide students the opportunity to hear and see the new structure, and to understand its meaning and its usage, before asking them to produce it? Most language teachers are concerned with what their students are able to do with language, namely how well they can perform communicative tasks. And most of these tasks require students to produce or output language, in other words, to write and speak. If we care so much about language output, shouldn't we invest more time in language input? Researchers have presented convincing arguments for the need and the means for providing students with the opportunity to systematically process new language, be it lexical (Krashen and Terrell 1983) or grammatical (VanPatten 1996). VanPatten, for example, argues that language learners are "limited capacity processors;" that is, they have just so much time in their working memory to attend to how the grammar is related and used. If students are required to attend to grammar for its meaning before they have to produce it, aren't they then in a position to use it more effectively when asked to do so?

This said, what does it mean to input grammar? To input grammar is to allow students the opportunity to make form-meaning relationships. By having to attend to the meaning of a given structure and how it is used, students have the opportunity to process it at a deeper semantic level. Look at Examples 1 and 2 below:

Example 1

Communicative goal: Students will report on what they did last night.

Essential grammatical explanation: First-person or *yo* preterite forms almost always end in *–é* or *–í,* like in the verbs *estudié, miré televisión, comí, fui.* One exception is *hice,* as in *hice la tarea.*

Possible input activities:

-The class follows a written text read to them by the teacher. *Anoche cené con mi familia, escuché música, leí un libro, miré un poco de television, y me acosté temprano.*

-The teacher asks the class: *¿Cierto o falso? Anoche fui a una discoteca (falso), escuché música (cierto), me acosté tarde (falso)....*

Note: Additional input activities would be provided.

Example 2

Grammar for grammar's sake goal: Students will learn the preterite.

Grammatical explanation:

The simple past tense in Spanish is called the preterite. The forms of the preterite for the *–ar, –er, –ir* verbs, and irregular verbs, are....

First exercise:

-After explaining how to conjugate the forms of each declension, the teacher (T) says to the class (C): "Repitan las formas del pretérito que digo...

     T: Yo hablé

     C: Yo hablé

     T: Tú hablaste

     C: Tú hablaste

     ...."

When we compare the two examples, we see that Example 1 gives students the opportunity to hear the first-person singular preterite forms and to begin to make connections between the forms (e.g., *é* and *í*) and their meaning (*yo*/past). The true/false input activity in the first example asks students to respond whether or not their teacher did a particular activity. For this activity students hear the *yo* verb forms, but do not produce them, and the only thing they are asked to say is *cierto* or *falso*. In other words, they are exposed to the forms and have to demonstrate comprehension of their meaning, but they do not have to produce them. In contrast in Example 2, the first thing students have to do is repeat preterite verb forms after their teacher. Students can successfully do the exercise, such as repeat after the teacher, yet may not know what they are saying.

Below is a series of input activities for the communicative goal of describing another person's daily routine. (The activity types are based on Lee and VanPatten 1995, pp. 104-113.)

To input the new verbs and vocabulary surrounding daily routines, a series of pictures of a student engaged in different activities is shown. The teacher describes each numbered picture shown: *"En la foto número uno Ana se levanta temprano. Después en la foto dos se viste. Luego en la foto tres desayuna cereal con leche. Y en la foto cuatro, sale de la casa....."* After presenting the series of pictures to the class, the teacher, would want to follow with a series of comprehension questions.

> T: ¿En qué número de foto desayuna Ana cereal con leche?
> C: Dos.
> T: ¿En qué número se levanta temprano?
> C: Uno.

Note that students are asked to respond using language with which they are already familiar, in this case numbers. They are not asked to produce the new grammatical feature (i.e., third-person singular verbs).

Similarly, students may be asked true/false questions about the series of pictures presented. Here again in order to answer the questions, students need to comprehend the meaning of the new grammar, but they are not required to produce it:

> T: ¿Cierto o Falso? En la foto número dos, Ana va a la
>   cocina.
> C: Falso.
> T: En la foto número cuatro sale de la casa.
> C: Cierto.

Once students have heard the new grammatical feature enough to be able to produce it, they can be asked either-or questions or open-ended questions, respectively:

Either -or question:
> T: En la foto número diez, ¿Ana estudia o almuerza?
> C: Estudia.

More open-ended question:
> T: ¿Qué hace Ana en la foto número siete?
> C: Hace ejercicio.

Students should also have the opportunity to experience these grammatical items in writing. Some of our students are visual (vs. auditory) learners and learn better when language is presented to them in written form:[1]

Match the item in column A with the logical item from column B.

Ana...

A	B
1. ___ se levanta	a. en la cafetería.
2. ___ desayuna	b. en la biblioteca.
3. ___ estudia	c. a las siete.
4. ___ almuerza	d. cereal con leche.

---

[1] Although the focus of this book is on the development of oral communication, several examples of written Spanish are provided here as it is believed that these will also help students with their language development.

Students can also be asked to order (say, from 1-6) each daily activity according to the order in which Ana, the person described, does them:

Ana...
___ almuerza
___ desayuna
___ se viste
___ se levanta
___ se cepilla los dientes
___ sale de la casa

The examples above provide students with both aural and written input. With the exception of the either-or and the open-ended questions (e.g., *¿Trabaja o hace ejercicio Ana?* and *¿Qué hace Ana en esta foto?*, respectively), students are asked to demonstrate comprehension of the new grammatical items, but are not asked to produce them. (For more examples of these "structured input" activities, see Lee and VanPatten 1995 [Chapter 5] and VanPatten 1996 [Chapter 3].)

Here again the suggestion is that each "new" grammatical feature be presented in a series of input activities to students, thus providing them the opportunity to develop familiarity with its meaning, form and usage before requiring them to produce it.

Below are examples of textbook production or output activities converted into input activities.

Example A.
This example is adapted from a college-level Spanish textbook. In a chapter on publicity and media careers, the future tense and its morphology are introduced. The original activity requires students to do an exercise in pairs, with one partner making *resoluciones* by conjugating the verbs given in the infinitive into the future tense, and the other partner listening, e.g., *hacer ejercicio > Haré más ejercicio, trabajar > Trabajaré menos.* This is a production exercise, yet it can easily be changed into an input activity. Keeping the theme of *resoluciones*, the teacher (T)

could read to the class (C) a series of statements of his or her possible resolutions, with the class guessing whether or not each statement is a genuine resolution of the teacher:

> T: Voy a leer una serie de oraciones. Indiquen si cada una representa una resolución mía o no….Trabajaré menos.
> C: No.
> T: ¡Correcto! No trabajaré menos; ¡trabajaré más! Miraré menos televisión y leeré más revistas.
> C: Sí, es cierto.

Another modification on the above *resoluciones* activity would be that instead of reading statements to the class, the teacher could provide students a series of statements for them to read. Again, students would be asked to guess whether each statement represents a true resolution of their teacher.

> ¿Resolución o no? ¿Cuál de las siguientes resoluciones haría tu profesor(a)?
>
> | | Sí | No |
> |---|---|---|
> | 1. <<Empezaré un nuevo trabajo. | ☐ | ☐ |
> | 2. <<Viajaré más. | ☐ | ☐ |

As a follow up, the teacher would ask the students to identify which statements they thought represented the teacher's resolutions, and which did not.

In both modifications described above, students would have an opportunity to experience the future tense (in the first-person singular) via input activities before having to produce it themselves.

Example B.

This example is also adapted from a college-level Spanish textbook. The theme of the textbook chapter is student schedules. The grammatical focus is the introduction of the structures *tener que* + infinitive and *ir a* + infinitive. (Students have already learned the days of the week.) The book shows a seven-day calendar in which the plans for the week of a person named Amanda are written (e.g., *lunes—escribir una composición para la clase, salir con Pablo; martes—llamar a Rosita, leer la lección para historia*). The first exercise asks students to immediately produce the new grammatical structures, for example:

> T: ¿Qué tiene que hacer Amanda el lunes?
> C: Tiene que escribir una composición.
> T: ¿Qué va a hacer el lunes?
> C: Va a salir con Pablo.

For an input version of this activity, the teacher could ask students questions that do not require them to produce the new (*ir a* + infinitive and *tener que* + infinitive) grammatical constructions, for example:

> T: ¿Qué día tiene que escribir una composición
>   Amanda?
> C: El lunes.
> T: ¿Cuándo va a salir con Pablo?

By modifying the way questions are asked, students hear the new structures and experience how they are used. As students answer with language they already know (days of the week), they may be freer to attend to the meaning and usage of the new grammar.

Just as students may need to experience vocabulary in a meaningful way before they are asked to produce it (see Chapter 3), so too do they need to experience a grammatical future in an input-based, meaningful way before they are asked to produce it. With a little practice, teachers can learn to modify their textbooks to include grammar-as-input activities.

PROACTIVE, RESPONSIVE, AND STUDENT-INITIATED GRAMMAR INSTRUCTION

Language teachers who support the middle-ground view that grammar should be taught in support of communication are usually both proactive and responsive in their approach to grammar instruction. "Proactive" refers to identifying the grammatical features that students are likely to need in order to carry out a particular communicative goal; and "responsive" refers to using student-produced "data" or utterances to give them corrective feedback. "Student-initiated" grammar instruction is grammar information that a student actively seeks when engaged in a communicative activity.

It is easy to be **proactive** with beginning learners in that most grammar information you present them is "new." From your grammar explanations to your input activities, you as the teacher are being proactive about the new grammar in anticipation of the communicative goal you have set for your students. Yet even when dealing with previously taught or "recycled" grammar with higher level students, it is wise to be proactive. On a lesson on the city, for example, the communicative goal may be to "explain to your partner how to get to the city library. Your partner will trace the route you describe on his or her map." In order to perform this activity, students need to use *tú* commands. Students are also likely to need *estar* + locative in order to talk about the location of the partner and the city buildings. Although students may have recently studied *tú* commands or the use of *estar* with location, it is judicious to be proactive and revisit those points with the class. No teacher should assume that since students studied a grammatical feature last week or last semester or last year, that they have "mastered" the feature. By being proactive and reteaching this information, students are more likely to use the grammatical information to carry out the communicative activity more accurately. And since this information is necessary to carrying out the stated communicative goal, students are more likely to pay attention to it.

Another example of proactive grammar instruction may deal with giving an oral presentation on what students believe life will be like in the year 2050. The grammar necessary to speak on this composition topic includes being able to use constructions such as *Creo que* + future tenses *(e.g., Creo que viajaremos en naves espaciales)*, and *Dudo que* + present subjunctive verbs (e.g., *Dudo que   haya tanto crimen*). The teacher could also be proactive in reminding students to be careful with subject/verb agreement, and with number/gender adjective agreement.

In short, proactive grammar instruction consists of providing students the structural tools that they will need to attain a communicative goal.

Responsive grammar instruction is providing students structural feedback on the language needed to carry out a communicative goal. This feedback is provided "after the fact," and its purpose is to focus student attention on what linguistic items should be improved upon. As mentioned in Chapter 1, some researchers and theorists argue that exposure to input alone does not assure grammatical accuracy, and that student output may prompt corrective feedback that may help students to achieve accuracy (e.g., Swain's Comprehensible Output Hypothesis, 1985). Responsive grammar instruction helps to guide students from point A—where they are—in hopes that they will progress to point B—where they should be. This type of instruction is usually provided after a communicative activity is completed.

In the above-mentioned example of giving a presentation on what students think life will be like in the year 2050, responsive instruction could involve providing the entire class or individual students with several pieces of grammatical information. This information would be what the teacher identifies as most helpful to improving a student's speech. Whereas one student may receive the feedback: *¡Ojo! con la concordancia de género, p.ej., con la palabra* 'nave'; another may receive: *Cuidado con los usos del presente del subjuntivo después de cláusulas de duda, p.ej. Dudo que..., No creo que....*

The following classroom activity illustrates an example of both proactive and responsive grammar instruction. The communicative goal is for students to share and later identify the most interesting things they have done in their lives. First, students are to write out 3-4 statements, which may be true or false. Before doing this, students are afforded proactive grammar instruction by the teacher who explains. "In order to talk about things I have done, one needs to use the present imperfect. The present imperfect of the first-person singular is formed with *he* + past participle, for example: *He viajado a Chile.* Students are then given one to two minutes to write their statements. Later, the class is divided into two teams, with one member of each team reading his or her statement, and the other team guessing if the item read is true or false. Teams alternate reading and guessing. For each item correctly identified, that team earns a point. The team with the most points "wins" applause or bonus points, (T = Teacher, S1= Student 1 from Team A), for instance:

S1:	He escalado las Himalayas.
T:	¿Cuántos del equipo B dicen que es cierto? (*Show of hands*) ¿Cuántos dicen que es falso? (*Show of hands*) La mayoría del equipo B dice que es falso.
T to S1:	¿Es cierto o falso?
S1:	Es falso.
T:	¡Un punto para el Equipo B! Ahora, ¿quién del equipo B desea leer su declaración?

Afterward, the teacher asks the class to comment on the most interesting things their classmates shared; and to comment on the biggest lies. Once the communicative goal is met (i.e., students successfully identified the most interesting things they have done in their lives), the teacher reviews several of the present perfect constructions produced by the students. She points out the correct forms and the inaccuracies produced during the activity: *He roto una promesa* (no *rompido*), *He escrito una canción* (no *escribido*). This is, of course, an example of responsive grammar instruction. Responsive grammar instruction may or may not be planned for on the part of the teacher. Based on the "data," namely the language that students produce in speech or in writing, the teacher may decide if responsive grammar instruction is warranted, and of what it should consist.

In addition to proactive and responsive grammar instruction, there is grammar instruction in response to *student-initiated* questions. This occurs when a student is actively involved in a communicative activity. In contrast to traditional grammar instruction, students find themselves in meaning-driven activities in which they themselves recognize the need for grammatical knowledge. Several "real-life" examples of student-initiated grammar instruction are:

a. In a pair activity, students are asking questions of one another to find out their personal history. A student asks the teacher: *"¿Cómo se dice* I was born, *fui nacido?"*

b. Students are working in small groups and have been assigned the task of describing their favorite celebrity. Group members are to listen and identify the celebrity, based on the description given. While describing Cameron Diaz, a student says: *"Ella es alta, guapa y ella tiene pelo rubia.* Ms. Smith, is it *pelo rubio or rubia?"*

c. Students are working with a partner to describe various weather scenes. A student asks: "Do you say *Lo está lloviendo* or just *Está lloviendo?"*

d. Students working in small groups are brainstorming a draft of a letter to the president of Mexico about their environmental concerns. One student asks *"¿Cuándo necesita la palabra 'que' acento y cuándo no necesita acento?"* Another asks: *"¿Qué se dice, 'Creemos es importante que..'* o *'Creemos que es importante que...'."*

If a student asks a question, and the question relates to the communicative activity at hand, then he or she deserves focused grammar instruction. Some language researchers and teachers call these student-initiated requests for information "teachable moments." These moments are spontaneous, and cannot be planned for. Teachers need to be alert to these occasional moments, as this kind of grammatical instruction is likely to make a lasting impression because it fills a student's self-identified need. And on occasions when several students ask very similar questions, it is probably appropriate for the teacher to do whole-class instruction.

(For more information on "focus on form" activities, in other words, grammar moments that arise in the context of communicative activities, see volumes edited by Doughty and Williams 1998 and Lee and Valdman 2000.)

LEARNING THROUGH CLEARLY ARTICULATED GOALS

Our approach to grammar requires that students be participants not only in their own learning, but also in the "meta-learning" that surrounds it. In other words, there should be no mystery about the grammatical purpose embedded in a communicative activity. Just as the communicative goal of an activity is made explicit for students (e.g., working in small groups, discover who has the most ambitious or interesting goals for the future), the grammatical goal (use future verb forms to talk about future plans) should be made explicit as well, and a brief lesson on the forms of the future would be in order to draw students' attention to the kinds of forms they will be producing (proactive instruction). Similarly, the follow-up phase of the activity, in which students report on their partners' future plans and the class votes on which plans are the most ambitious or interesting, could also include a grammatical segment (responsive instruction). With clearly articulated goals, we make communicative activities more purposeful while helping students become more aware of their own learning.

TEACHER EXPECTATIONS: GRAMMATICAL ACCURACY, LANGUAGE LEVEL, AND ACTIVITY COMPLEXITY

Below are several teacher expectations we would like to share related to our professional experience and our position on the role of grammar in the communicative classroom.

•**When engaged in communicative activities, students of all language levels will make mistakes.** When concentrating on what they are saying or writing, students have difficulty achieving and maintaining grammatical accuracy. (And by the way, don't most Spanish teachers whose native language is English have occasional difficulty in Spanish maintaining correct adjective gender and number agreement, particularly in rapid conversation?)

•**The more complex the communicative activity, the more likely students will make mistakes.** Students asked to "name three activities you did yesterday" (and use preterite forms) will make far fewer mistakes than students asked to "describe the funniest experience you've ever had" (while using the preterite and the imperfect).

•**Some grammatical mistakes are "performance" errors (i.e., we "know" the correct rule and form, but nonetheless make a mistake while in the throes of communication), and not "competence" errors (i.e., we do not know the correct rule).** "Performance" errors or "slips of the tongue" do not need to be corrected by the teacher. "Competence" errors may warrant grammar instruction if the teacher feels it will fulfill a student's communicative need.

•**Some grammatical features are easier to acquire than others.** Students learn early on, for example, that most nouns in Spanish end in –*o* or –*a*. It takes them much longer, however, to acquire accurate noun/adjective agreement. And by the same token, whereas students quickly learn to use or overuse *ser* (*Juan es simpático; Ellos son hablando español*), it takes them an extremely long time to acquire all the uses of *ser* and *estar* (VanPatten 1987).

•Given comparable communicative tasks, students will make more errors in speech than in writing. Whereas writing affords students the opportunity to choose and edit their language, such is not the case in spontaneous speech. Therefore it is not surprising to find a higher number of errors in learner speech. This said, students nonetheless need to be taught to be both producers and editors of their own language production.

•Don't think that students will learn all the grammar correctly before they can use it meaningfully. Research has shown (e.g., Ellis 1986; Larsen-Freeman and Long 1991; Lightbown and Spada 1993) that grammatical accuracy develops over time. Just as it takes children learning their first language time to develop linguistic accuracy (e.g., L1 Spanish children who say *"yo sabo"* before they learn to consistently say *"yo sé"*), our students need the time and the opportunity to develop their linguistic system.

•Grammar instruction should be given at appropriate times in the lesson. (See the discussion above and Chapter 3).

SUMMARY

In this chapter we have made a case for the role of grammar instruction in the communicative classroom. After presenting two opposing viewpoints—no explicit grammar instruction and "grammar for grammar's sake"—we have presented our middle-ground position. This position asserts that the question confronting language teachers should not be if we should teach grammar, but rather what grammar to teach and how. And it is the communicative goals which determine what grammar content to teach.

We also have raised the issue of appropriate grammatical instruction, that is, depending on communicative goal, what grammatical information would be essential, what "extra," and what non-essential. Whereas incomplete information may prevent students from carrying out a communicative activity, too much information may in fact distract them from the goal.

Another topic addressed is that of grammar as input. It is our view that students need to have the opportunity to hear and see new grammatical features before they are asked to produce them. Several suggestions are offered for providing this grammatical input.

We have also outlined three types of grammar instruction: proactive instruction, which occurs before students do a communicative activity and can be planned for by the teacher; responsive instruction, which occurs in response to the "data" or utterances students make and may be spontaneous; and student-initiated instruction, which are special "teaching moments" when students indicate their individual grammatical needs relevant to the communicative task at hand. In a similar vein, we assert that it is important to clearly articulate both the communicative goals and the embedded linguistic goals of a given activity, so that the student has a better awareness of the purpose of the activity and what he or she should be learning from it. And in an attempt to "cover more of the (grammar) bases" we have provided a short list of teacher expectations that briefly addresses such issues as grammatical accuracy, and complexity of communicative task.

The questions posited at the beginning of the lesson were:

Question 1: What role should grammar play in the
communicative classroom?
  a. Grammar has no explicit role in the classroom.
  b. Grammatical knowledge and mastery is the goal of language learning.
  c. Grammar should be taught insofar as it supports communicative goals.

Question 2: How is the answer in Question #1 manifested in the Spanish classroom?

    a. Through rich exposure to Spanish in a variety of contexts, students will learn grammar. It is not necessary, then, to teach grammar.

    b. Spanish grammar is taught and practiced so that students gain mastery over the linguistic system.

    c. **Grammatical goals are embedded in communicative activities, and the teacher seizes opportunities for relevant grammatical instruction.**

We are hopeful that you now have a good understanding of why our answers to both chapter-opening questions are, of course, "c".

APPLICATION ACTIVITIES FOR REFLECTION AND DISCUSSION

1. In your own words, what does it mean to "teach grammar in service of communication?"
2. Assuming your students will be asked to carry out the following communicative activities, what essential grammar information would you teach them (or reteach them) beforehand?
   a. Students are asked to identify the top three things they would do if they were president of the United States.
   b. Working in pairs, one partner is asked to describe the sports actions he or she sees in a picture, with the partner drawing the actions described.
   c. Students are asked to write a description of their dream house or dream date.
   d. In a mock job interview, students are asked to describe their past job experiences.
3. In this chapter we mentioned a concern with the common textbook practice of requiring students to produce a grammar point immediately after introducing it. For each situation below, identify one or two grammar input activities which would precede each communicative activity.
   a. Working in dyads, students have a city map. Using informal *tú* commands, one partner needs to direct the other to get from point A (e.g., *la biblioteca*) to point B (e.g., *el museo*).
   b. Students working in small groups are asked to identify their group's choice for best movie ever made. Using superlatives and comparisons, students are asked to explain to the class why their chosen movie is so deserving.
4. We have discussed grammar instruction that is proactive, responsive, and student-initiated. What type of grammar instruction is taking place in the following scenarios?
   a. In small groups, students are discussing the advantages and disadvantages of the city versus the country. The

teacher hears several students say *el ciudad*. She briefly interrupts the class to say, for example:

T: *A propósito, clase, se dice **la** ciudad. La palabra ciudad es femenina.*

 b. Students are working in small groups on a weather report they will present to the class tomorrow. One student raises his hand and asks the teacher:

  S: *¿Se dice 'hace nubes' o 'está nublado'?*

 c. The teacher has asked students to write an essay describing the most significant event in their life. Before writing, students are given a review on the uses of the preterite and the imperfect, for instance, the preterite is used to describe events, and the imperfect is used for background information.

5. A colleague of yours comments that he is confused how his Spanish 4 students make few mistakes on *por* and *para* fill-in exercises, yet make many mistakes with *por* and *para* when writing and speaking. What would you like to say to him regarding grammar, teacher expectations, and communicative language teaching?

ACTIVITY DESIGN AND LESSON PLANNING IN THE COMMUNICATIVE CLASSROOM

Please choose the most appropriate response .

Question 1: If not grammar, the focus of the language class is __.
    a.   to transmit and receive messages
    b.   instructed language use
    c.   content-based learning
    d.   learning scenarios
    e.   All of the statements are correct.

Question 2: Ideally, teachers should use Spanish in the classroom __.
    a.   50% of the time, because sometimes students need something repeated in English
    b.   75% of the time; use English to make sure that students understand instructions
    c.   almost 100% of the time; reserve English for rar communication breakdowns

Question 3: The term "task-based instruction" refers to instruction based on __.
    a.   interaction among students
    b.   goal-oriented pedagogy
    c.   a means and an end
    d.   a purpose for language use
    e.   All of the statements are correct.

INTRODUCTION

The purpose of this chapter is to describe the focus and instructional design of a communicative language class. The communicative classroom is often contrasted with a grammar focused language class. The principal difference between the two is that the former is driven by a series of communicative goals and the latter is driven by a series of grammatical forms. As a vantage point from which to view the communicative syllabus, it may be helpful to review the tenets of a grammatical syllabus.

What does it mean to say that a syllabus is "driven by a grammatical focus"? Comments such as the following typically accompany grammatical syllabi:

1. "In the first semester we will cover the present indicative,the periphrastic future (*ir a* + infinitive), and the simple future tenses. The second semester covers the preterite and the imperfect, the conditional, and the subjunctive."
2. "When do they get the subjunctive?"
3. *"Por* vs. *para"*
4. "Students must learn all the grammar before they can communicate."

The goal of a course with this type of focus is to study on a predetermined schedule all the major verb tenses, their respective conjugations and uses (e.g., present indicative, preterite, imperfect, conditional, present subjunctive, imperfect subjunctive) and the linguistic structures (e.g., definite articles, indefinite articles, direct object pronouns, indirect object pronouns) in Spanish. This goal is motivated by the belief that knowledge about and practice with the nuts-and-bolts of the language must necessarily precede opportunities to express oneself with the language; and that without said knowledge of the grammatical rules, communication and meaningful language use are either problematic or not possible at all.

Many syllabi and textbooks fall under this umbrella description. Typically, a lesson following such a syllabus opens with a dialogue or reading containing a number of examples of a particular grammatical item (e.g., the present indicative). This reading is then followed by a series of exercises in which the students (a) fill in the blank with the appropriate form of the grammatical item:

Juanita _____ *(hablar) tres lenguas*

(b) rewrite sentences or phrases to incorporate or reflect a modification associated with a specific item:

José tiene el libro (nosotros) → *Nosotros tenemos el libro*

(c) answer comprehension questions derived from the information in the reading or dialogue:

¿Dónde están Juanita y José? → *Juanita y José están en Guadalajara.*

Although the purpose of this last type of exercise may appear to be to learn new information about the characters in the dialogue or reading, the underlying aim of the contextualization (i.e., the travels of Juanita y José) is a vehicle for the presentation, memorization, repetition, substitution, and transformation of the focal grammatical items.

As we saw in Chapter 2, however, whereas grammar instruction in the communicative language classroom is a means to learning how to communicate, it is not an end in itself. If the grammatical forms are not the primary guiding focus of the classroom (and subsequently the guiding outline of the materials), the logical question that arises is *what is the focus?* How do we construct and organize a communicative syllabus for the language classroom?

In this chapter, we examine the following topics: the focus of the communicative syllabus (*If not grammar, then what?*); the use of Spanish in the classroom; the pedagogical elements that constitute a communicatively oriented syllabus; and task-based instruction (i.e., instruction whose focus is language use to achieve specified goals). We discuss how this type of instruction is organized, what it looks like (including examples), and how it organizes a syllabus. We then look at its relationship to a learning scenario as outlined by the *Standards for Foreign*

Language Learning (National Standards in Foreign Language Education Project 1996).

FOCUS OF INSTRUCTION

Consider the following questions: Why do most people want to learn another language? If you speak more than one language, why did you learn the second (or third) language? Some may say they learned another language because they grew up in a bilingual environment or moved to a place where a different language was spoken. Many others, however, would say that they decided to learn a second or third language to: (a) speak the language, (b) understand the language when spoken to, (c) write the language, or (d) read articles or books in the language. Not many people would say that they learned another language because they had an insatiable desire to conjugate the imperfect subjunctive of verbs that end in *–ar*, or that they longed to be able to recite the list of direct object pronouns. Most people learned another language to express ideas, understand messages and in the case of misunderstanding or a lack of understanding, arrive at mutual comprehension. In short, they wanted to be able to communicate (Savignon 1997).

If the primary focus of the class is to learn to communicate in Spanish, rather than talk about the structure of the language (i.e., verb forms, pronoun systems, etc.), this same focus informs us about how to design and structure what we do in the classroom (e.g., how to interview, make a request, negotiate, and describe). We may say that the goal of the language class is to learn how to carry out specific communicative tasks rather than to produce specific grammatical forms.

In a grammatically focused syllabus, the unifying element of each lesson and unit is one or more grammatical structures, verb forms, or paradigms (e.g, the present indicative, *saber* vs. *conocer,* imperatives). Typical study topics associated with grammatical and communicative syllabi are shown in Figure 1.

Figure 1. Sample topics in grammatical vs. communicative syllabi

Grammatical	Communicative
Present indicative	Summer actvities
	(*¿Qué haces durante el verano?*)
Preterite	Telling stories
imperfect	(*La experiencia que más miedo me causó fue...*)
Si clauses	Imagining the impossible
	(*Si fuera rico (rica), yo ...*)

In comparison to the grammatically oriented syllabus, the focus or unifying element of each lesson in a communicatively oriented syllabus is a theme or topic in the real world (Ballman 1996, 1997, and 1998; Krashen and Terrell 1983; Shrum and Glisan 2000). Such topics may include cultural or personal themes: *La geografía del Ecuador, ¿Qué comemos?, La historia de los Reyes Católicos, ¿Qué carreras hacemos?*. The topic or thematic question of the lesson suggests the activities in which students use language for a purpose. The topic or theme also determines the vocabulary and the grammatical structures that the students will need to successfully learn about the topic. Thus, explicit language instruction, whether it be about vocabulary or grammar, can be said to be at the service of the topic and of the communicative goal of the lesson.

USE OF SPANISH IN THE CLASSROOM

A note about the amount of Spanish to be used in the classroom appears in order at this point. As has been pointed out, the goal of Communicative Language Teaching (CLT) is to teach students to express themselves, understand others, and to request clarification or express lack of comprehension to others—all in Spanish. With such a goal, it is imperative that Spanish be the primary language used in the classroom. It is only through comprehending and processing meaningful messages in Spanish that students receive the material they must have to develop their own ability to produce language. Furthermore, the instructor is the primary supplier of what Spanish sounds like and how it works as a language. Students rely on the instructor's use of language to learn how to process and produce their own. Depriving them of that vital element is in essence starving their language system.

You may be saying to yourself at this point, "Well, I speak Spanish most of the time but every once in awhile I have to speak in English for a number of reasons." The scenarios that follow exemplify issues raised by the use of English in the Spanish classroom.

Scenario A: The instructor speaks Spanish while conducting language activities and interacting with students, but regularly gives instructions, calls roll, explains assignments and conducts other bureaucratic duties in English. Although the use of English may be necessary at times, what does the routine use of English for one purpose and Spanish for another implicitly communicate to the students? Obviously, the instructor feels that to be understood, some types of information can only be transmitted in English, the students' native language. Unfortunately, the message conveyed by this two-tiered system is that English is the more important language.

Scenario B: The instructor says something in Spanish (e.g., a sentence, a test item, an oral reading) and then almost immediately repeats the same utterance in English. What message does this behavior send to students? While thinking about this question, ask yourself the following: If students know that all information given in Spanish is going to be repeated immediately in English, why should they pay any attention to the message in Spanish? Repeating the same message in English and translating from Spanish to English sends students the message that there is no reason to pay attention to what is said in Spanish and, therefore, that the Spanish may be ignored.

Scenarios A and B illustrate ways in which unintended messages may be conveyed to students by behaviors that honestly and innocently are meant to help them. The misleading assumption that underlies this type of assistance is that a combination of Spanish and English will help students learn Spanish faster. What we have seen, however, is that these assisting behaviors may actually suggest to students that they need not pay attention to the messages conveyed in Spanish.

The teacher's use of Spanish in the classroom not only serves as input to the students as they develop knowledge of the language, but also reinforces student use of Spanish in the classroom. As Ballman (1998) states, "teachers need to ensure that students use the target language and stay on-task during learner-centered activities" (p. 99). To do so, teachers need to be explicit about the expected use of Spanish in the classroom and must also set an example. Use of Spanish by the teacher does not guarantee that students will use Spanish when working in pairs or small groups, of course, but the teacher who uses Spanish consistently models the behavior expected of the students and encourages them to follow suit. In addition, the teacher's Spanish provides the students with examples of how the language sounds and is used. (For discussion on "teacher talk" and how it influences classroom interaction, see Chapter 5.)

PRESENTATION OF VOCABULARY (COMPREHENSIBLE INPUT)

One primary building block of any theme-related Spanish lesson is the vocabulary with which the students must be familiar to engage the material in the lesson. The ways in which new vocabulary is presented may ultimately determine the students' success in carrying out an activity. Vocabulary learning is important for two reasons. The most obvious is that an increasing knowledge of words in a language is the immediate measure of knowledge of the entire language. A second and not so readily noticeable value of vocabulary learning is rooted in the relationship between vocabulary familiarity and ease in communicating.

Language students are "limited capacity processors" (VanPatten 1996), which means that they pay attention only to so many things at a time. There are many different elements in the language vying for students' attention. Each word in a language, for example, is composed of a number of different types of information (i.e., how it sounds, how it is pronounced, how it modifies other words, how it can be modified, what it means, and where it can appear in a sentence). Given their limited processing capacity, students cannot simultaneously process all these different types of information about a new word. As a learner's knowledge about the language grows, it becomes easier not only to pay attention to more words, but also to deal with the many types of information contained within and related to individual words.

Have you ever witnessed a Spanish discussion activity in which one or more students begin in Spanish but gradually move to English, their first language, while perhaps referring to dictionaries or resorting to word-for-word translations? Why do those students feel the need to rely on these resources, rather than to continue in Spanish? The primary reason may be the lack of familiarity with vocabulary and the different types of information related to vocabulary as described above. In other words, the students reach the limits of what they can attend to and begin to rely on support mechanisms related to English. Being aware of how students process new vocabulary and their limits to do so informs us about how to most effectively introduce new words and phrases.

The following scenarios from actual Spanish classrooms illustrate a number of ways in which new vocabulary is frequently presented. Read the following scenarios and think about whether you have ever witnessed or participated in a similar episode.

Scenario C:

Teacher:	Voy a leer unas palabras relacionadas con el tema de la lección. Repitan Uds.
	Telenovela
All students:	Telenovela
Teacher:	Emisor
All students:	Emisor
Teacher:	Anfitrión
All students:	Anfitrión

In this scenario, the class is beginning a lesson about the influence of television in contemporary culture. The instructor goes down a list of new vocabulary items, word for word, and after pronouncing each word, waits while the entire class chorally repeats it. What is the pedagogical goal of this exercise? Do the students come away with an increased knowledge of the meanings of these new vocabulary items? Probably not, but they possibly do have a heightened awareness of what the words sound like and how they are pronounced.

Scenario D:

Teacher:	Como una introducción al nuevo capítulo, vamos a leer esta lista de vocabulario. Matthew, ¿puedes empezar, por favor?
Matthew:	(reading *sacerdote*) Er, uh, sakerdot (reading *Inquisición*) Uh, inkwizishun.[1]

In this scenario, the teacher plans to use new vocabulary words as a point of entry into the lesson. For that purpose, the teacher calls on a student to read aloud this list of unfamiliar words. The question that arises here is the same as before: What is the pedagogical goal of this exercise? Why is the student's pronunciation so inaccurate? What are the other students doing while the student is trying to read the words aloud? Are students

---

[1] The renderings in the student's speech above are meant to be phonetic, indicating how the speaker is pronouncing the words.

expanding their knowledge of Spanish vocabulary? It seems doubtful that student knowledge about word meanings is increasing but rather, as was the case in Scenario C, the class is being exposed to an inaccurate rendering of the new vocabulary items. Why do you suppose the student Matthew is producing the new words the way he is? What knowledge is he accessing in order to fulfill the instructor's request?

Scenarios C and D are two examples of well-intentioned activities that one could witness in many Spanish classrooms at the beginning of a new lesson or chapter. While the idea is presumably to prepare the students for new material by acquainting them with the topic-related vocabulary, in both cases the recitation of vocabulary items amounts to individual or choral pronunciation exercises. It is quite likely that students complete these types of exercise with very little idea of what the new terms mean. Compare these two scenarios with the two (Scenarios E and F) that follow.

Scenario E: Picture file
Teacher: Voy a leer unas palabras y expresiones que se asocian con el clima y el tiempo. Miren los dibujos que están asociados con cada expresión.
En este dibujo, hace frío. (*Shows a drawing labeled A of a child in the snow.*)
Está nublado. (*Shows a drawing labeled B in which there are many clouds.*)
Hace sol. (*Shows a drawing labeled C in which a family in sunglasses is at the beach. Next, teacher posts drawings A, B, and C on the board in front of the class.*)
¿En qué dibujo está nublado?
Students: B.
Teacher: En este dibjuo hace sol y la gente está en la playa.
Students: C.

In this scenario the teacher is presenting expressions about how to talk about weather. In the first part of the presentation, the teacher articulates a weather-related expression and then simultaneously presents an illustration of that condition. Each picture has been labeled beforehand (A, B, and C). During this presentation the students listen to the new vocabulary items and observe the representative illustrations. Following the initial presentation, the teacher displays the pictures, describes a weather condition, and asks the class to indicate which picture is being described. What is the goal of this activity? What are the students doing? When the students produce language, what do they produce and what does that tell the teacher?

The purpose of this activity is to introduce the class to the new vocabulary through prepared pictures that illustrate the target vocabulary items. A picture file is one means by which the teacher converts the presentation of a list of vocabulary items into good comprehensible input (Krashen and Terrell 1983; Lee and VanPatten 1995). That is, students make direct connections between the words and phrases articulated by the instructor (who is providing language input and exemplifying the pronunciation of the items) and then meaning as depicted in the illustrations. In addition, the accuracy of the item/picture associations serves as a comprehension check to both the instructor and the students.

The scenario below illustrates yet another way to focus learner attention on the meaning of new vocabulary by combining movement with the use of a picture file:

Scenario F: Total physical response – TPR

   Teacher: Hoy estudiamos el vocabulario que se usa para hablar de lo que se encuentra en los cuartos distintos en la casa.

(*With an appropriate photo*) Aquí tengo la foto de un sofá. El sofá lo encontramos generalmente en la sala. (*Hands the photo to a student in class.*)

(*With another photo*) Aquí tengo la foto de una cama. La cama la encontramos en el dormitorio. (*Hands the photo to another student.*)

	(With another photo) En esta foto se ve un escritorio. El escritorio lo encontramos en el dormitorio o en el estudio. (Hands the photo to a student.) Levántense si no tienen la foto del sofá.
Class:	(All students rise except the one student with the appropriate photo.)
Teacher:	Bien. Ahora siéntense.
Class:	(All students sit down.)
Teacher:	Levántate si tienes la foto de la cama.
Class:	(All remain seated except the student with the appropriate photo, who stands up.)

In this scenario, the teacher is presenting vocabulary used to talk about different pieces of furniture as well as the rooms in the home in which one would expect to find them. As the teacher names each item, illustrated by the photo, students make the direct connection between the vocabulary word and the object. The students also receive input about how each vocabulary word is pronounced. Each photo is then given to a different student in class. Following the presentation, the instructor directs all students except the student in possession of the photo of the sofa to stand up. The students are then instructed to sit down. Subsequently the student with the photograph of the bed is asked to stand. What is the goal of this activity? What do the students produce?

The activity described in scenario F is based on the method of Total Physical Response (TPR) according to which the meaning of new vocabulary is associated with actual physical movement (Asher 1977). As an example of this method students' attention is directed to make an immediate association between a target item (in this case, the word *sofá* or *cama*) and what it means. Students do not produce the new word, thereby freeing their attention to focus on meaning. (For more examples of TPR activities, see Harper and Lively 1991; Krashen and Terrell 1983, pp. 76-78; and Lee and VanPatten 1995, pp. 52-54.)

The comparison of scenarios C and D with scenarios E and F makes clear the differences between exercises that focus students' attention on the pronunciation of novel vocabulary items and activities that focus their attention on the meaning of those items. Notice in particular that whereas scenarios C and D prompt students to immediately produce unfamiliar vocabulary items, scenarios E and F prompt students to attend to the meaning of the unfamiliar items, without requiring that they produce the target items. That is not to say that students passively watch the presentation. They indicate their comprehension of the input either by identifying the correct visuals (e.g., Teacher: *¿Cuál es la foto del gato: A o B?* Class: *B*) or by carrying out some physical activity with the visuals (e.g., Teacher: *Los que tienen una foto de un gato o un perro, levántense.*) Which of the activities do you think would result in more vocabulary learned? Why? Whereas the students in scenarios C and D may be learning about Spanish pronunciation either chorally or individually, the students in scenarios E and F are learning not only how the new words sound, as the teacher pronounces them, but also what they mean by the associating the new words and expressions with related pictures and actions. Notice as well how the activities in scenarios E and F focus the students' attention on both pronunciation and meaning of the new vocabulary without overloading their processing capacity.

As a final note about these types of activities, we are not passing judgment on the exercises or activities illustrated in the four scenarios in this section. Each type of activity serves a different purpose. Our intention is to highlight the purpose of the different activities. Certain activities focus students' attention on the production of a particular item or series of items, as in scenarios C and D, whereas others focus their attention on processing language for meaning, as in scenarios E and F.

ACTIVITY TYPES AND DESIGN

You may be saying to yourself, "My students and I regularly do activities in class in Spanish. Is my teaching communicatively oriented?" It very well may be. As we have already seen, two important components of CLT are use of the target language (Spanish) in the classroom and activity design. In this section we discuss a number of activity types that prompt meaning-focused language use in the classroom. We begin with an example of an interview activity, an activity type that appears in a number of language texts. We then discuss information gap activities designed to encourage opportunities for negotiation between participants. Finally we introduce the concept of task-based instruction as a means of facilitating real communicative language use in the classroom.

INTERVIEW ACTIVITIES

Interview exercises are often labeled as communicative activities because of the type of interaction they are assumed to foster. Following the presentation of a particular grammatical point, many current textbooks include activities in which students are paired up to use a series of questions to interview each other. The following is an example of one "interview a partner" activity from a college-level Spanish textbook.

Entrevista. With a partner, ask each other the following questions. Be prepared to report back to the class.

> MODELO: E1: ¿Qué estudias en la universidad?
> E2: Estudio español....

1. ¿Qué estudias en la universidad? 4. ¿Dónde trabajas?
2. ¿Qué idiomas hablas bien? 5. ¿Cuándo regresas a la clase?
3. ¿Viajas mucho o poco? 6. ¿Te gusta bailar?

Although this type of activity appears to create a meaningful context for language use, two questions about the activity arise about the instructions and the real purpose of the activity. Although the instructions say to "be prepared to report back to the class," what are students going to report on and how? Students will be more focused on this activity if they are asked to do something concrete with the information they gather (e.g., fill out a chart, complete a paragraph, compose an outline). In addition, as one looks at the questions given, one must ask if the questions relate well, one to the other (e.g., *¿Cuándo regresas a la clase?* and *¿Te gusta bailar?*), or if they really intended to practice *–ar* verbs? Compare the design of the interview exercise above with the activity below:

Entrevista.

Step 1: Pair up with a classmate and fill out the following form as you interview him/her about his/her class schedule, language, travel, and work experience. Below are some questions you may use during the interview. (*Be sure to ask follow-up questions for other details you find interesting. You will need this information to describe your classmate's schedule later on.*)

¿Qué estudias en la universidad? / ¿Qué idiomas hablas bien? / ¿Viajas mucho o poco? ¿Adónde? / ¿Dónde trabajas?

Mi compañero/a de clase

Nombre: _____

Materias: _____

Idiomas:_____

Trabajo:_____

Other:_____

Step 2: Using the information gathered in Step 1, complete the paragraph below to share what you learned about your classmate to the rest of the class.

Mi compañero/a de clase

Mi compañero/a, _____ (nombre),
estudia _____, _____ y
_____. Habla _____. Trabaja
en _____. Viaja _____
y le gusta ir a _____.

Although this peer interview activity guides students to gather the same types of information as the first version, notice how the design incorporates a form to be completed as the students fulfill the purpose of gathering information about their classmates while conducting the interview. The questions, taken from the first version, become tools to be used for information gathering. Returning to the question of how students will report back their findings to the class, the modified version of the activity includes a report template that students will use to facilitate meaningful summary of their findings. This addition provides a formatted purpose to the interview.

INFORMATION GAP ACTIVITIES

Interview-type activities like the first version of the one shown above offer opportunities for the transmission and reception of messages, but do they prompt authentic language use? In the course of real and authentic communicative exchanges, all participants have opportunities not only to transmit and receive messages but also to clarify transmissions and request rephrasing or repetition in the event of real or perceived lack of understanding. When students are responsible for filling out a form with specific information, that communicative need pushes them to ask for clarification or repetition. In other words, the accountability that is built into the second version of the interview activity gives the activity greater communicative value.

Brooks (1992) criticizes the traditional interview exercise in favor what he calls jigsaw tasks or information gap activities that provide opportunities not only for message transmission and reception but also for negotiation (i.e., message clarification, requests for repetition, comprehension checks). Information gap activities provide learners with different but complementary pieces of information that must be combined to successfully accomplish the goal of the activity. This type of activity requires that students work together as a team to solve a puzzle that cannot be resolved without meaningful interaction between them.

In the following example of an information gap activity, participant A needs flight information to complete travel plans for company employees and participant B is the representative at an airport.

(A)

You are responsible for the travel arrangements for your company's sales representatives in Caracas. You have to check on the status of the flights for the following employees who should be leaving today. The airport has been having problems due to a pilot strike. You need to find out the departure times and the gate numbers so you call airport information. Use the following phrases:

¿Sabe Ud...?   *¿Hay retraso?*

¿De qué puerta...?   *¿Me puede decir a qué hora sale...?*

Your partner will begin.

	Aerolínea:	Vuelo		Hora	Puerta:
Roberta Morales	United	632	Miami	_____	_____
Carmen Rey	Lan Chile	301	Santiago	_____	_____
Wilson Lerma	Iberia	465	Madrid	_____	_____

| Víctor Malatesta | Avianca | 345 | Bogotá | ____ | ____ |
| Jesús Coello | Lacsa | 203 | San José | ____ | ____ |

(B)

You work at the information desk at the airport in Caracas. Look at the following departure board on your computer screen and give the appropriate information. Phrases that may be useful to you include:

¿Cuál es el número del vuelo?   *¿En qué línea...?*
Sale a las...   *Sale de la puerta número...*
No sé, no hay información

You begin by answering the phone and saying:

Aeropuerto Maiquetía, buenos días.

SALIDAS

Aerolínea	**Vuelo**		**Hora**	**Puerta**
Avianca	345	Bogotá		
Avianca	582	Cartagena	13:15	6
Iberia	465	Madrid	Retraso	10
United	632	San Juan / Miami	Retraso 8:35	3
Lan Chile	301	Santiago	9:15	7
Lan Chile	420	Lima / Santiago	14:35	22
Lacsa	203	San José	Retraso 10:00	11

(Adapted from Garner, Rusch, and Domínguez 1991, p. 6)

The design of this example requires that the two participants meaningfully interact in Spanish in order to bridge an information gap. Participant A has the incomplete travel itineraries of five employees for a company in Caracas.

Participant B possesses the flight schedules of seven flights for different destinations from the Aeropuerto Maiquetía. Again notice how this activity not only prompts information transmission and reception (i.e., the times and gates of five flights), but also negotiation (i.e., information requests, clarification requests, and possible repetition requests and comprehension checks) between the two speakers.

Activities similar to the sample shown above may include schedule completion, map completion, form completion, or drawing comparison, to name but a few. (See Garner et al. 1991 for many more excellent examples of information gap activities designed for learners of Spanish at four different levels.)

TASK-BASED ACTIVITIES

One guideline that may be used to ensure communication in each class session, lesson, and unit is that in each activity students should have a reason for doing something in Spanish. In other words, the goal of the class is that students use the target language to carry out a particular task. We adopt the following definition of task, as articulated by Lee (2000):

> A *task* is (1) a classroom activity or exercise that has (a) an objective attainable only by the interaction among participants, (b) a mechanism for structuring and sequencing interaction, and (c) a focus on meaning exchange; and (2) a language learning endeavor that requires learners to comprehend, manipulate, and/or produce the target language as they perform some set of workplans. (p. 32)

Based on this definition, task-based instruction is characterized by three components. First, task-based instruction is learner-centered in that successful completion of a task is only possible as a result of student-to-student interaction. Examples of this type of interaction include compiling and comparing real and authentic information known only to the individual learners

76

involved (e.g., national origin of grandparents, number of times per week meals are eaten in restaurants, individual preferences for indoor or outdoor activities, travel plans for the upcoming semester break). Second, task-based instruction requires an activity that focuses on a meaningful exchange of information on the part of the participants. Examples of this type of activity include an interview, census, survey, or opinion poll. Finally, task-based instruction guides participants through a series of predetermined steps that culminate in a concrete representation of the information shared or gathered. Examples of this type of representation include filling in a chart, drawing a diagram or a map, completing a paragraph, or writing a quiz based on the information gathered.

A sample task-based lesson activity illustrates the three components described above. In a lesson about food and eating habits, a class wants to answer the question *¿Cómo es la dieta típica del estudiante típico en nuestra clase?* For the first task of an activity designed to answer this question, the students form pairs and interview one another with the questions shown in Figure 2 below.

Figure 2. Example questions for task-based activity on eating habits

1. ¿Cuántas veces comiste en casa esta semana ____?
      el desayuno   _____
      el almuerzo   _____
      la cena   _____
2. ¿Cuántas veces comiste en un restaurante esta semana ____?
      el desayuno   _____
      el almuerzo   _____
      la cena   _____
3. En un desayuno típico en casa, ¿qué comes? (*Escribe un cheque al lado de todas las comidas indicadas.*)
      ___ pan tostado ___ huevos   ___ tocino
      ___ jugo   ___ leche ___ cereal
      ___ café   ___ _____

4. En un desayuno típico en un restaurante, ¿qué comes?
   (*Escribe un cheque al lado de todas las comidas indicadas.*)
   ___ pan tostado   ___ huevos   ___ tocino
   ___ jugo   ___ leche   ___ cereal
   ___ café   ___ _____

5. En un almuerzo típico en casa, ¿qué comes? (*Escribe un
   cheque al lado de todas las comidas indicadas.*)
   ___ un sandwich   ___ una hamburguesa
   ___ zanahorias   ___ jugo   ___ leche
   ___ papas fritas ___ café   ___ un refresco .
   ___ _____

6. En un almuerzo típico en un restaurante, ¿qué comes?
   (*Escribe un cheque al lado de todas las comidas indicadas.*)
   ___ un sandwich ___ una hamburguesa ___ zanahorias
   ___ jugo   ___ leche   ___ papas fritas
   ___ café   ___ un refresco ___ _____

This sample activity satisfies the first component of task-based instruction requiring student-to-student interaction in that successful completion depends upon learners gathering real information from one another about their eating habits. The information about where they eat (questions 1 and 2) and what they eat (questions 3-6) is known only to and can be provided only by them. This activity also satisfies the second component, that the activity focuses on meaningful information exchange, in that the learners use the questionnaire above to interview one another.

In the second task of this sample activity, each pair of students joins another pair of students to form groups of four. Each group elects a secretary and, using the information from the first task, compiles the information about eating habits by filling out the chart shown in Figure 3.

Figure 3. Example chart for group information compilation on diets

	Casa	*Restaurante*
Número de desayunos:		
Número de almuerzos:		
Número de cenas:		
Número en un desayuno típico:	___ pan tostado ___ huevos ___ jugo ___ café ___ leche ___ tocino ___ cereal ___ ___	___ pan tostado ___ huevos ___ jugo ___ café ___ leche ___ tocino ___ cereal ___ ___
Número en un almuerzo típico:	___ sándwich ___ hamburguesa ___ zanahorias ___ jugo ___ leche ___ papas fritas ___ café ___ un refresco ___ ___	___ sándwich ___ hamburguesa ___ zanahorias ___ jugo ___ leche ___ papas fritas ___ café ___ un refresco ___ ___

¿Dónde se come más frecuentemente?_____
¿En cuál de los dos sitios se come más variedad de comida para
el desayuno? _____
¿para el almuerzo? _____

The second task in this sample activity satisfies all three
components of task-based instruction. According to the first
component, the activity is learner-centered in that the students in
groups work together to accomplish the goal of the task. The
activity satisfies the second component in that they must
exchange meaningful information about each group member to
complete the task. Finally, the activity satisfies the third
component in that each group has a chart in which the
information gathered from individual students is compiled upon
completion of this task. That information will be used by each
group to address the questions below the chart (e.g., *¿Dónde se
come más frecuentemente?, ¿En cuál de los dos sitios se come
más variedad de comida para el desayuno?*). The next step is to
have the class nominate a secretary to use the same chart above
to compile the information from each group and, by dividing the
total number of responses by the number of students in class,
lead the class to answer the original question, *¿Cómo es la dieta
del estudiante típico de la clase?*

One important aspect in the design of a syllabus based on
task-based instruction deals with the roles of the teacher and the
students. In many language-learning activities, discussion
questions provide opportunities for language use and thus,
presumably, for communication. However, have you ever
witnessed the case in which a discussion activity boils down to
an exchange between the teacher and one or two of the best and
most motivated students, while the other 15 or 20 students sit and
watch? Although this type of interaction admittedly provides an
opportunity for communicative interaction for the parties
involved, it does not do so for the other students in the
classroom. Communication should not be a spectator-sport.

Task-based instruction is an example of what has been referred to as "learner-centered" as opposed to "teacher-fronted" instruction (e.g., Ballman 1998). In teacher-fronted interactions, the instructor is the singular focus of all the learners and all information exchange involves the instructor. Although typical classroom lectures and dictations are two prime examples of teacher-fronted activities, so-called discussion activities may also fall into that classification if, as described above, the flow of information is essentially between the instructor and individual student(s). In learner-centered interactive activities, the students rely on and interact with one another for completion of a task.

In learner-centered communicative instruction, pairs or small-groups of learners are given a particular task that requires them to work together in Spanish in order to attain a specific goal. To ensure that student interaction stays in Spanish and stays on task, the following four guidelines should be followed:

1. the purpose of the activity is made clear to the students;
2. the activities are designed incrementally so that one builds upon another;
3. the learners have preparatory language and/or linguistic support necessary to carry out the activity; and
4. the students have a specified time limit in which to carry out the activity or task.

The first guideline provides the students with a purpose for the activities and a framework within which to carry them out. (e.g., Teacher: *En esta actividad vamos a contestar la pregunta: ¿cómo es un fin de semana típico del/la estudiante típico/a?*) This framework establishes the reason for the activity, its relation to the lesson or unit, and some idea of what to expect within the activity. The second guideline suggests that there be a logical progression between each of the activities in a task. Prior to attempting to address the question above, for example, students would need to carry out the following: *Actividad A: ¿Qué haces los sábados?, Actividad B: Un sábado típico, ¿qué tiene en común tu horario con el horario de tu compañero?, Actividad C:*

¿Qué haces los domingos?, Actividad D: Un domingo típico, ¿qué tiene en común tu horario con el horario de tu compañero? According to the third guideline, students should be given an opportunity to review the vocabulary and grammar they will need to carry out an activity (e.g., *Actividades: ir a la iglesia, a la sinagoga, ir a la piscina, ver televisión, asistir a un concierto*). Finally, according to the fourth guideline, a time limit is clearly established by which the particular activity or task is to be carried out. A time limit helps to keep students on task.

Two caveats are in order regarding pair or small-group learner-centered activities in the communicative classroom. We do not advocate the sole use of pair and small-group work to the exclusion of teacher-centered activities. As we saw earlier, teacher-centered activities are essential because it is the teacher who provides input, thereby modeling what the language means, how it sounds, and how it is used. In addition, the teacher modifies language to make it comprehensible to students. Scenarios E and F above, for example, are teacher-fronted activities. The incorporation of pair and small-group work is not an end in itself, but rather a means to increase individual student opportunities to communicate (Long and Porter 1985).

A second note about learner-centered activities relates to how students model their interactions in this type of activity. Research has shown that students model the interaction in their pair or small-group work according to the types of interactions they have experienced during teacher-fronted activities (Brooks 1990; Kinginger 1990). If the regular teacher-fronted activities in class are grammatically focused drills and exercises, students in learner-centered activities tend to model that type of activity as well, regardless of the intended purpose of the activity. As a consequence, students may convert an interview activity, for example, into a verb paradigm drill. If, however, the routine teacher-fronted activities are focused on meaningful message exchange, the odds are increased that the same type of behavior will take place in the learner-centered communicative activities. (For more discussion on classroom interaction, see Chapter 5.)

TASK-TO-TASK SYLLABUS DESIGN

In this section we discuss a syllabus based on task-to-task instruction and examine how the goals of the syllabus determine the steps to link a series of tasks, one to the other. As we saw in the previous section, individual tasks provide a structured format for student-to-student communication to attain a particular goal. One productive framework for communicative lesson planning is to tie together a series of individual tasks together in relation to a specific lesson topic. The string of tasks eventually culminates in a culminating task drawing on elements focused on in previous tasks. Figure 4 illustrates the relationship between intermediary and culminating tasks.

Figure 4. Order of intermediary and culminating tasks

Task A + Task B + Task C → Culminating Task

Tasks A, B, and C are smaller, intermediary tasks that students will need to do in order to carry out a larger, culminating task. The culminating task generally takes place at the end of a lesson. The feature that unifies a string of activities may be a topic or thematic question such as, for example, *¿Cómo es tu familia?* An example string may help to see how these different task types are related.

Sample Sequence of Tasks

One topic that lends itself well to a beginning Spanish class is, of course, family. It is safe to assume that all participants in a class are familiar with the essentail concept of families and how they are organized. In this sample string, the culminating task is to interview someone about his or her nuclear family in order to draw and label his/her family tree, as represented in Figure 5.[1]

---

[1] Students who do not wish to talk about their own families should be given the option to discuss a famous or dream family.

Figure 5. Family lesson culminating task

Task A + Task B + Task C→   Culminating Task

To interview
someone and
draw his/her
nuclear family
and label with
names, ages,
and professions

What types of intermediary tasks does the beginning student of Spanish need to do in order to be successful with the culminating task? The language (vocabulary and grammar) that students need to be familiar with includes:

a. the terminology used in Spanish to talk about the nuclear family (e.g., *padre, madre, padrastro, hermano, medio hermano*);

b. the verb forms used with *tú* (e.g., *tienes*) and *él/ella* (e.g., *¿Trabaja?*) to ask questions of a classmate about his family and to later report on the information learned;

c. interrogative words used in questions (e.g., *¿Cómo se llama tu madre?*, *¿Cuántos años tiene?*); and

d. the vocabulary related to other related types of information (e.g., age, marital status, profession).

One could imagine a hypothetical week-long series of lesson plans that would look something like the following, as illustrated in Figure 6.

Figure 6. Family intermediary tasks and culminating task

Task A	+ Task B	+ Task C	→ Culminating Task
To ask a classmate to identify the members of his/her nuclear family	To report the ages of a classmate's family members	To discover the professions of the parents of the two classmates' family	To interview someone and draw his/her nuclear family and label with names, ages, and professions

---

To complete Task A, for example, students would have to be able to ask another classmate questions about his or her nuclear family. To do so would require students to be use interrogative words to ask questions, and to able to use the verb forms associated with *tú* and *él/ella*. To successfully complete Task B, students would need to be familiar with the vocabulary associated with numbers (say, 1-100) and with age expressions (e.g., *tener años*). Finally, Task C would require that students be familiar with the vocabulary associated with professions, to be able to once again ask questions of classmates, and to report on others' professions.

Three observations deserve highlighting at this point. For starters, notice how the nature of the culminating task determines the types of intermediary tasks that precede it, in terms of both general vocabulary items and grammatical items. Second, observe how the focused presentation of specific grammatical items is incorporated into a lesson plan. Whereas under the rubric of a grammatical syllabus, a lesson plan would present all of the forms of the present tense as one segment of a daily lesson plan, here specific forms (e.g., the forms associated with *tú* and *él* or *ella*) are in focus to interview a classmate and report on what he or she says about the members of his or her family. A third observation about this type of task-based lesson plan involves student progress, both from the individual student's perspective as well as from the teacher's vantage point. In particular, how does the student or the teacher know when the task has been successfully completed? Both students and the instructor know the activity's goal has been met when the student can carry out the specific task assigned (e.g., ask a classmate the ages of his or her family members; and finally, interview someone in class and complete a subsequent representation of his or her family tree). Of course, the information gathered will also be reflected in tests and assessment materials, to be discussed in Chapter 4. This type of lesson plan makes it easy to know when one has successfully accomplished the goal of a particular activity.

(See Appendix A for two sample strings of five-day lesson plans on the topic of family. The first string is for a beginning level Spanish class and the second string is for an Advanced Placement [AP] level Spanish class).

LEARNING SCENARIOS AND *THE STANDARDS FOR FOREIGN LANGUAGE LEARNING*

The task-based instruction format proposed above within a CLT syllabus parallels the development of learning scenarios as described by the *Standards for Foreign Language Learning* (National Standards in Foreign Language Project 1996; Phillips and Terry 1999). Accordingly, learning scenarios facilitate lesson planning so that a number of the *Standards for Foreign Language Learning*, subsumed by the Five C's of Foreign Language Study—Communication, Cultures, Connections, Comparisons, and Communities—are met in content-focused and cross-disciplinary study (Guntermann 2000; National Standards in Foreign Language Education Project 1996).

The task-based instructional framework illustrated above in Figure 6 is compatible with the notion of the learning scenario. A sample learning scenario illustrates the similarities between these two lesson frameworks.

LEARNING SCENARIO: TRAVEL PREPARATION

A local high school Spanish class is preparing to travel to Costa Rica during midyear break. Students will be staying with Costa Rican families in different parts of the capital city, San José. In preparation for the trip, the students want to know what kind of clothes to take (based on what is fashionable and what kinds of outings they may make), what the weather is like there, and what type(s) of foods and dining habits they may expect while in Costa Rica. The students divide themselves into three groups. Each group takes responsibility for one of the three types of information (clothing, weather, food and eating habits). Under guidance and supervision, each group researches its topic utilizing everything from printed resources available at the library to television programs, Web resources, and international chat rooms. Subsequently, each group of students prepares an oral and visual presentation to inform their classmates about the information found in preparation for the upcoming trip.

This learning scenario addresses the following goals according to the *Standards*:

1.1 Interpersonal Communication: Students engage in conversations, provide and obtain information, express feelings and emotions, and exchange opinions;

1.2 Interpretive Communication: Students understand and interpret written and spoken language on a variety of topics;

1.3 Presentational Communication: Students present information, concepts, and ideas to an audience of listeners or readers on a variety of topics;

2.1 Practices of Culture: Students demonstrate an understanding of the relationship between the practices and perspectives of the culture studied; and

4.2 Culture Comparisons: Students demonstrate understanding of the concept of culture through comparisons of the cultures studied and their own.

Although it is not immediately a part of the scenario, the trip to Costa Rica will also address:

5.1 School and Community: Students use the language both within and beyond the school setting.

This sample learning scenario, illustrated in Figure 7, may be analyzed as to how it fits the task-based instructional model.

Figure 7. Elements of the lesson and culminating task in travel preparation learning scenario

A	B	C	D	E
Vocabulary	**Grammar**	**Grammar**	**Cultural Information (Resources)**	**Culminating task**
Clothes, weather, food and eating habits	1st person plural present, 3rd person plural present	Passive *se* and Impersonal *se*	Articles, TV, Web resources, Chat rooms	Group presentations on the three topics

The culminating task (E) is the oral presentation that each group makes to the rest of the class. Students listening to each presentation will not only use the information presented to carry out the immediate goal of filling out a chart, completing a paragraph, preparing some type of summary or a similar activity, but will also use what they learn to prepare themselves for the actual trip. Each of the three groups (e.g., clothes, weather, and foods and eating habits) has a separate set of questions to ask, all of them subsumed by the information needed by the other members of the class to prepare for the upcoming trip to Costa Rica.

Working backwards from this final task, the resources (D) to be used by students while preparing their presentation may vary depending upon the questions that either (a) the students choose to address in their presentation, or (b) the instructor assigns. Similarly, depending on the level of the class, the teacher may choose to provide the groups with a previously selected series of resources (e.g., maps, catalogues, magazines, books, and Web addresses) or the students may be capable of searching for these materials on their own. These resources can be used in order to identify relevant cultural information.

The sections indicated in A, B, and C assume a string of related input (and/or review) activities and output activities. The vocabulary in A on clothing, water, and foods and eating habits will be needed not only by each of the groups for their respective presentations, but also by the rest of the class on the trip. The second element of the leson with which learners will need to be familiar deals with grammar. As illustrated in Figure 7 above, B addresses two grammatical topics that students will need to know, not only as presenters in their respective groups but also as audience of the same presentations, the first-person plural in the present indicative (e.g., *Necesitamos pantalones y camisas para el viaje en la selva.*), and the third-person plural of the present indicative (e.g., *Los costaricenses no comen mucha carne pero sí comen mucho arroz con frijoles negros frecuentemente.*). A second element of the activities found in C may also be included on the use of the passive *se* and the impersonal *se* to talk about cultural generalizations in preparation to travel abroad (e.g., *Se usan tenedor y cuchillo para comer fruta en Costa Rica*). As mentioned above, element D refers to the use of resources to find pertinent cultural facts.

These two analyses of this sample Learning Scenario (one based on the *Standards* and the other based on the organizing principles of task-based instruction) reveal how the goals of both types of syllabi or lesson plans are not only met by the same design but are related to each other. In fact, the guiding principles of task-based instruction as outlined here (i.e., vocabulary activities + grammar activities + information source activities → culminating task) facilitate and provide an underlying formula for incorporating the *Standards*-based learning scenarios into the communicatively oriented Spanish classroom.

SUMMARY

In this chapter we have compared the focus of a grammatically oriented syllabus with a communicatively oriented syllabus. We have seen how the focus of instruction in a communicative syllabus may be motivated and guided by a theme and a specific series of questions to be addressed by the learners. The relationship between the elements in a task-based communicatively oriented syllabus (vocabulary activities, grammar activities, and communicative tasks) have been outlined. The importance of the use of as much Spanish as possible for all purposes (bureaucratic purposes and teaching activities) has also been proposed, noting the implicit messages conveyed by the use of English in the classroom. We discussed traditional interview exercises, information gap activities and task-based instruction, in which learners use Spanish for the purpose of completing a task or attaining a goal. Finally we have seen how learning scenarios as proposed by the *Standards for Foreign Language Learning* follow a design parallel to those proposed in task-based instruction.

Returning then to the three questions posed at the beginning of this chapter, we can see that the answer to the first question: If not grammar, the focus of the (communicative) language class is indeed e) All of statements are correct. While students are learning to transmit and receive messages (a), they are also receiving instructed language use (b), and content-based learning (c), through carefully designed learning scenarios (d). In response to the second question: How much Spanish should the instructor optimally use in class?, although the best response would be almost 100% (c), we acknowledge that at times the

90

level will be closer to 75%, allowing for the use of English to make sure instructions are understood (b). That said, we have seen how the response 50%, use of Spanish with repetition of items in English (a), can implicitly dissuade students from paying attention to messages conveyed in Spanish. Finally, in response to question 3, we have seen that the answer is (e) All of the statements are correct. Task-based instruction is: instruction based on interaction between learners, goal-oriented pedagogy, and both a means and an end, all of which provide the classroom with a purpose for language use.

APPENDIX A

Below are sample lesson plans for two different levels of communicative-language teaching oriented Spanish classes. The topic in both sets of lesson plans is the family. The first set of lesson plans is for a beginning-level Spanish class. The second set of lesson plans is for an Advanced Placement (AP) Spanish class.

BEGINNING LEVEL*

Day 1
   A. Nuclear family vocabulary (Picture file activity)
   B. Average family size in the U.S. and several Spanish-speaking countries
   C. *Task: ¿Son Uds. típicos o no?* Students compare average family size of their respective group with that of average family size of U.S. and several Spanish-speaking countries.

Day 2
   A. Spanish royal family, nuclear
   B. Concept of *monarquía parlamental*
   C. Instructor's nuclear family (description and family tree activity)
   D. Formation of possession (__ *de* __)

E. *Task:* Students in pairs write questions based on Spanish royal family and instructor's family which are later asked of class.

Day 3

A. Famous Hispanic families (description and picture files)
B. Meaning and uses of possessive adjectives (e.g., *su, sus*)
C. Interrogative words and question formation reviewed
D. *Task:* Teams of students alternate asking questions of a volunteer student in order to discover the identity of a famous family

Day 4

A. Extended family vocabulary (Instructor family tree)
B. Spanish royal family, extended
C. Concept of extended family in Spanish speaking world (magazine article)
D. Concept of family used in advertising (w/samples from magazines)
E. *Task:* Students identify similarities and differences in the representation of family in English and Spanish-language advertisements

Day 5

A. Teacher illustrates use of two last names in many Spanish-speaking countries
B. Average age of marriage in U.S. and in several Spanish-speaking countries (magazine article activity)
C. *Task:* Students identify themselves using two last names, and react to the practice. Later, students identify and compare the average age at marriage of the class and their friends to the U.S. average and the average in several Spanish-speaking countries.

Day 6

A. *Task:* Step 1--students interview a classmate in order to draw his or her family tree and label it.
B. *Task:* Step 2--students complete a paragraph comparing the classmate's family with the average family size of another country.

C. *Task:* Step 3--students compare their classmate's family with the Spanish royal family or with another well-known Hispanic family. Information gathered in the three steps is turned in to the teacher for evaluation.

* (Adapted from Ballman 1997)

ADVANCED PLACEMENT LEVEL*

Day 1

A. Teacher reviews nuclear/extended family vocabulary (Picture file activity). Teacher reminds students about adjective agreement.

B. *Task:* Information-gap activity: partners with different information work together to supply information about same family tree

C. *Task: Extended family trees* After teacher reminds students to be careful with adjective agreement, students in pairs describe their respective family trees while partners draw the trees.

D. *Task:* With reading about Hispanic families, pairs generate a list of characteristics of urban vs. rural life before sharing with class

E. Homework – students write a 1-page composition comparing their own family with families in reading; students read about changing Hispanic families. Teacher reminds students to be careful with adjective agreement and with the conjunction *que*.

Day 2

A. Audio recordings of interviews: students identify families as rural or urban

B. *Task:* In pairs, one partner reads a definition, other partner identifies word from list

C. Brainstorm activity about rural/urban family characteristics

D. Reading activity in small groups on changing U.S. and Hispanic families. *Task:* Each group summarizes for the class the group's assigned section. Class discussion follows.

E. Homework – students write composition on changes over last 50 years in U.S. families. Teacher reminds students of construction with noun clauses that require use of the subjunctive, and of uses of the imperfect indicative.

Day 3

A. Audio interviews with Hispanics about perceptions of U.S. families
B. *Task:* Vocabulary team game (Define the word)
C. *Task*: Brainstorm about Hispanic family reading from Day Two. Then, one partner read the other's compositions, commenting on its content. Next, partners help edit 1-2 paragraphs for above-mentioned grammar points
D. Movie*:* Class sees first-half of Spanish movie about family-related topic
E. Homework: Students edit their own compositions.

Day 4

A. *Task:* Brainstorm about portion of movie shown on Day Three
B. Movie: Class sees second half of Spanish movie
C. *Task:* Peer-editing of composition for language
D. *Task:* Students in small groups choose a side for tomorrow's debate on *La familia de hoy vs. la familia del pasado* and prepare their arguments. Teacher explains how debate will be evaluated. Also, everyone is expected to participate and students will receive a group grade.

Day 5

A. *Task:* Each small group presents its debate arguments.
B. Class discussion: Summarizing debate, readings, movie
C. Teacher leads class in reviewing target vocabulary, as well as important points of the reading and the movie.
D. Homework: Final editing changes to compositions due next day

*(Adapted from Ballman 2000)

APPLICATION ACTIVITIES FOR REFLECTION AND DISCUSSION

1. At the beginning of this chapter we discussed grammatical vs. communicative syllabi.
    a. Four examples of comments associated with grammatical syllabi (e.g., *When do they get the subjunctive?*, *Students must learn all the grammar before they can communicate*) are given at the beginning of this chapter. Can you think of two or more comments you have heard that might be included with these examples?
    b. Figure 1 on page 62 compares three topics from a grammatical syllabus with three parallel topics from a communicative syllabus, for example: (grammatical) *Si* clauses vs. (communicative*)* Imagining the impossible: *Si yo fuera rico (rica), yo....* Propose matching topics from a communicative syllabus for each of the following grammatical topics: (a) informal commands, (b) the future tense, (c) interrogative words, and (d) the conditional.
2. Find a section of "comprehension questions" following a dialogue or reading in a Spanish textbook. Is the purpose of these questions to check learner understanding or is there another agenda? (Hint: Look at the verb forms in the questions. Could you find answers to these questions without understanding the dialogue or reading passage?)
3. Figure 1 (p. 62) presents a list of topics that might be included in a communicative syllabus, for example, *¿Qué te gusta hacer durante el verano?* Select one of the topics in Figure 1 or propose one of your own and: (a) write three subtopics that could be included in a unit with your selected topic (e.g., *pasatiempos favoritos, tipos de trabajo*); (b) write a list of vocabulary items in Spanish that students would need to be familiar with in order to work with each subtopic (e.g., *viajar, nadar en el mar, ir a un parque de atracciones*); and (c) identify specific grammatical forms or structures students would need in

order to work with each subtopic (e.g., verb forms for *Uds.* to interview a classmate about what he or she does with her/his family, and verb forms of *nosotros* to report what I do with my family).

4. We recommend that teachers use Spanish almost exclusively in the classroom, for both classroom maintenace (e.g., calling roll and giving directions) as well as actual lesson activities. Why is it difficult to maintain consistent Spanish usage? How could this goal be made easier? In other words, what could teachers do to help put students at ease?

5. Scenarios C (p. 66) and D (p. 66) are examples of teachers using choral repetition and individual pronunciation activities to introduce new vocabulary. Some have suggested that teachers may lead these kinds of activities because they feel uncomfortable being the only ones speaking in the classroom. Review Scenarios E and F (on pages 67 and 68-69, respectively). In these scenarios is the teacher the only person participating? What are the students doing?

6. Scenarios E (p. 67) and F (p. 68-69) are examples of two ways (picture file and TPR) by which teachers can present new vocabulary to students by focusing attention on what the new words mean and not on the production of the new words. Can you think of other techniques or types of activities that can also be used to input vocabulary?

7. Describe a culminating task that you would expect students to carry out upon completion of a lesson on a chosen theme (e.g., Theme: summer vacation; Task: interview a classmate about what he or she did last summer and prepare an illustrative collage of those activities). Following the diagrams on family in Figures 5 and 6 (p. 84 and p. 85, respectively), what intermediary tasks would lead up to that culminating task (e.g., to ask a classmate three places he or she visited last summer). What vocabulary themes and grammatical topics would

the students need in order to accomplish each one of the tasks you list (e.g, the preterite forms associated with tú and with *él/ella*)?

EVALUATION OF ORAL COMMUNICATION IN THE COMMUNICATIVE CLASSROOM

Please choose the most appropriate response.

Question 1: What kinds of oral tests should we give?
    a. Speaking assessments should be done one-on-one with the teacher so that each student's performance can be evaluated independently.
    b. Because real-world speaking usually occurs in pairs or groups, oral tests should also be given to pairs or groups of students together.
    c. We should plan to use a variety of oral assessments to reflect the speaking activities in the curriculum.

Question 2: How should student performances on oral interaction tests be evaluated?
    a. Because speaking is a complex activity that consists of many parts, a single holistic score is most appropriate.
    b. Objectivity should be the teacher's first priority in evaluation, so a system like counting errors to arrive at a score is most appropriate.
    c. Because evaluation is a part of instruction, a system for scoring oral interactions that fits the teacher's goals for the test is most appropriate.

INTRODUCTION

Now that we have discussed the theory and practice of classroom communication, we move to the issue of assessment. The question that underlies this chapter and that provides a context for the specific questions above, is this: Given the time and effort inherent in testing oral communication skills, why do it at all?

Can't we just be content to assess students' progress and competence in the other skill areas, for which tests are considerably easier to design, administer, and score?

The short answer is no, we cannot leave speaking out of our testing program, even though the assessment of speaking skills can be difficult and time-consuming. Why not? Because if we take seriously the dictum to test what we teach, we must commit ourselves to assessing students' communicative abilities in Spanish. In the sections below, we first consider the reasons for testing in general and for evaluating speaking skills in particular. Then we discuss some important questions about the format and design of oral tests that are intended to both evaluate and promote communication in Spanish. Sample evaluation activities are presented as models for teachers to use and adapt in their own classroom assessments.

TESTING: THE NATIONAL CONTEXT

Testing is a fact of life in education, perhaps more so today than at any other time in recent history. Foreign languages are virtually absent from the large-scale national assessments, a fact due to the general position of languages as a peripheral, not core, component of most state (and, therefore, of most district and school) curricula. As a consequence, foreign language teachers may have greater freedom than their colleagues in other subject areas to design tests and other assessment procedures to reflect the priorities and content of their programs.

This situation, however, may be on the verge of change. In 1996, the document *Standards for Foreign Language Learning: Preparing for the 21st Century* was published; this publication was followed in 1999 by *Standards for Foreign Language Learning for the 21st Century*, which contained language-specific standards for nine languages, including Spanish and Portuguese. Almost all of the 50 states have foreign language curriculum frameworks based to some degree on the *Standards*, and test development efforts are underway or completed in several states (see http://www.ncssfl.org/state.htm for state reports on assessment efforts). The state of New Jersey now includes foreign language in its core curriculum and is committed to offering articulated and sequenced K-12 language instruction to all students, accompanied by an assessment program (New Jersey World Languages Curriculum Framework, 1999).

Foreign language is now included in national-level assessment efforts as well. As of this writing, the National Association of Educational Progress (NAEP) is preparing the first foreign language assessment in its 30-year history, which will be administered in two stages in 2003. The first stage will consist of an online questionnaire to a representative national sample of all twelfth graders to collect demographic information, experiences with foreign language learning both in and outside of school, attitudes about language study, and self-reported language abilities. The second stage will be an assessment of ability in Spanish for a sample of students in the first group (http://www.cal.org/flnaep/page3.html). As with all assessments in the NAEP program, the purpose of the foreign language assessment is to provide information to the public and to policy makers about the state of education and the status of reform efforts (http://www.cal.org/flnaep/page1.html). In the case of the Spanish NAEP, an important focus of the report will be to show the relationship between length of study of Spanish and achievement in the language. As we are all aware, this is a crucial issue in foreign language education and the efforts at the local level to provide longer sequences of language study.

Although the upcoming NAEP assessment will not report scores by individuals, schools, or even by states, it still has the potential to affect policies and practices in testing at state and district levels. The results of the NAEP assessments will receive national coverage, and the test questions and the underlying philosophy of the NAEP assessment will be widely disseminated. Both the Spanish NAEP and the state-level curriculum frameworks and corresponding testing projects are inspired by the *Standards in Foreign Language Learning*, particularly the focus on "communicative ability as [demonstrated in] authentic communication tasks" (http://www.cal.org/flnaep/page3.html). In the case of the Spanish NAEP, the assessment will include all four language skills, including interpersonal speaking. Students and a test administrator will engage in one-on-one conversational tasks, including a role play in which students will have the opportunity to demonstrate their knowledge of the language, apply their cultural knowledge and understanding, and appropriately use communication strategies (e.g., asking for clarification, showing concern for their comprehensibility).

The current efforts to respond, even in large-scale testing programs, to the emphasis of the *Standards* on authentic, interpersonal, task-based communication support the message of this book; that is, the invitation to Spanish teachers to concentrate their instructional energies on helping students develop their skills in these same areas. The new tests that are being developed in concert with the *Standards* will also provide teachers with ideas for their local, classroom-based assessments of communicative speaking skills.

WHY TEST? THE MANY PURPOSES OF TESTING AND ASSESSMENT

Before considering what or how to test, it is essential to articulate why we test; that is, the purposes that an evaluation is intended to serve. The content, format, scoring procedures, and even the weight given to the test will depend on the goals we hope to accomplish. What are the purposes for testing, and what implications do these purposes have for the types of tests we might develop?

PLACEMENT TESTS FOR NEW STUDENTS

Placement tests are used at the college level as an articulation device to assign incoming students to the course that best matches their current level of knowledge and skill. Secondary schools that draw students from a variety of Spanish programs or that are located in communities with mobile populations may use placement tests as well. Because the goal of a placement test is to match incoming students to a group of resident students, successful placement tests sample the main areas and principal emphases of the curriculum. In addition, score ranges for each course or level to which incoming students will be assigned are determined through a norming procedure: Current students take the placement test and their scores are used as the standard against which incoming students are judged.

Practical considerations may dictate some compromises in the content coverage of a placement test. For example, if entering Spanish students in a large university take the placement test the week before fall classes start, the test has to be scored and the results posted very quickly so that students may register for the appropriate course. This may mean that the speaking component of the placement test is reserved only for the most advanced students or for borderline cases, or that test formats include or are limited to multiple-choice questions. In these cases, it is important to monitor the performance of the entering students to assure that the decisions made on the basis of the placement tests are correct, even if the tests themselves do not reflect the content and orientation of the curriculum as well as the designers would like. Placement tests may need to be revised and renormed periodically if the curriculum undergoes major changes.

TESTS AS DATA TO ASSIGN GRADES

Perhaps the role of tests with which we are most familiar is that of providing teachers with information on student progress and achievement so that they may assign course grades fairly. It is generally accepted that we should test what we teach, but how do we design a testing program for our courses or programs that accomplishes this goal? As an example, let's say that we want to design a testing program for a third-year high school Spanish class.

The first step is to develop a detailed and accurate map of the content of the course. We are all sure that we know what we teach (content), how we teach (classroom activity types), and how much emphasis we give to each component. However, to be sure that our perceptions match reality, it is important to conduct an analysis of our curriculum, lesson plans, and teaching materials to create an accurate account of the content, approaches, and emphases of the course. The testing program should be a representative sample of the course content, approaches, and emphases. As a practical matter, it helps to keep in mind that not every evaluation activity has to reflect the whole course; this would be impossible. But taken as a whole, the testing program should allow students to demonstrate their progress and achievement in all significant aspects of the course.

To see how this might work in practice, we use an outline of the evaluation program of Intermediate Spanish I at the University of Iowa presented in Figure 1. This is a third-semester course that is taken by students whose background consists of high school Spanish courses, college Spanish courses, or a combination of the two.

Figure 1. Evaluation program for Intermediate Spanish I, University of Iowa

Chapter tests (5 @ 50 points each)	250
Reading quizzes (10 @ 10 points each)	100
Writing activities (5 @ 30 points each)	150
Web search activities (4 @ 10 points each)	40
Online chats with class members or other (5 @ 10 points each)	50
Bulletin board (on-line discussions, 10 contributions)	50
Midterm oral exam	50
Final exam:	50
oral component	50
written component	150
Workbook assignments to be turned in (6 @ 10 points each)	60
Class participation	50
TOTAL	**1000**

(Liskin-Gasparro 2001b)

In analyzing this evaluation program, it may be helpful to consider it from various perspectives. For example, we can sort the ways students accumulate points toward their course grade into two broad categories: graded activities that reward primarily participation and consistent effort (e.g., online chats, bulletin board discussions, workbook assignments, class participation), and those that reward mastery of the linguistic aspects of Spanish (e.g., chapter tests, final exam, and workbook assignments) or of their skill in speaking (e.g., oral exams). Alternatively, we can look at the weight given to the various language skills. Reading, for example, is evaluated in the frequent quizzes, the tests and final exam, and in the computer-mediated activities that involve reading as well as writing. If we note that the online chats share some features with speaking as well as reading and writing, we can see that speaking activities (online chats, oral exams, class participation) account for 20 percent of the final grade.

EVALUATION ACTIVITIES AS MOTIVATIONAL DEVICES

What makes students study hard and take their Spanish courses seriously? Some students are inspired by their love of the language, their desire to travel, or the realization that Spanish could be an important part of their future professional lives. For the majority of students, grades are a significant factor in their decisions about how to allocate their time and energy. We can take advantage of this reality by designing an evaluation program that focuses on the behaviors that contribute most to students' learning. For example, if we know that students devote more time and attention to their homework when there will be a quiz on that material, we can make sure that we schedule quizzes to coincide with a section of the course that requires students' focused and sustained attention. Similarly, if we stress oral communication in class but it corresponds to only a small percentage of the final grade, students will be less likely to treat it seriously. We all wish that our students were motivated by their love of Spanish but, unfortunately, this is not usually the case. We can, however, capitalize on students' practical orientation to course grades by using evaluation activities to help them allocate their study time appropriately, and focus on certain components of the course. In so doing, tests function as partners in student learning.

The term "washback" refers to the impact that tests have on teaching and learning. It is most often used in discussions of how high-stakes tests, such as those now administered regularly in several states in math and reading, change curriculum and teaching practices. When students' scores have important implications for school governance, teachers' salaries, and the like, the impact of these testing programs on teaching and learning can be enormous, and may result in a narrowing of the curriculum. We have seen in this short discussion of student motivation, however, that locally designed Spanish tests that correspond to communicative goals can have a positive washback effect on both students and teachers.

TEST FORMATS: CONSIDERATIONS AND PRACTICAL SUGGESTIONS

All teachers are familiar with the eternal tension between test formats and the time needed to score them. Tests in which students have to synthesize their accumulated knowledge and skill demand considerably more teacher time than those in which students fill in blanks, check boxes, or fill in bubbles on an electronically scored answer sheet. We all know that evaluating students' knowledge in communicative contexts is preferable to marking short answers right or wrong, but the pressures of time require us to make compromises. In this section we discuss ways of assessing students' Spanish performance communicatively, but in ways that do not take up inordinate amounts of time.

HADLEY'S (2000) MODEL OF TEST ITEMS AND TEST TYPES

Hadley (2000) presents a schema for analyzing the characteristics of a test item or activity. Her model allows us to judge the item or activity along two planes: the discourse of the stimulus material (i.e., the question), whether isolated sentences or sequential discourse; and the nature of the expected response, whether convergent (one right answer) or open-ended (many possible answers). Her model is presented in Figure 2..

Figure 2. Hadley's schema for assessing characteristics of test items

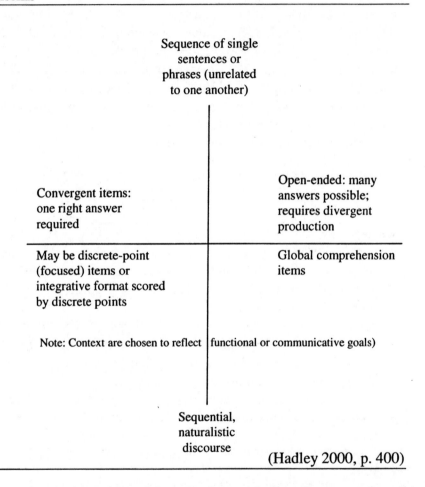

Sequence of single
sentences or
phrases (unrelated
to one another)

Convergent items:
one right answer
required

Open-ended: many
answers possible;
requires divergent
production

May be discrete-point
(focused) items or
integrative format scored
by discrete points

Global comprehension
items

Note: Context are chosen to reflect functional or communicative goals)

Sequential,
naturalistic
discourse

(Hadley 2000, p. 400)

To see how this schema can be used, we offer examples of test item or activity formats that correspond to each of the four quadrants of the graphic above. The upper left-hand quadrant describes items that are based on isolated sentences or phrases, with no relationship with what comes before or after; and there is only one correct answer possible. For example:

Example 1. A set of convergent-response grammatical items presented in isolated sentences

De viaje. Complete the following sentences using the correct form of the present indicative of the verb in parentheses.
1. Yo _____ (empezar) mi viaje el 2 de octubre.
2. Eduardo y Bárbara _____ (volver) en tren.
3. El camarero _____ (recomendar) el flan.
etc.

(Adapted from Renjilian-Burgy et al. 1999, p. 137)

Although the title of the test section points to a common context, the sentences are not linked together in a significant way. Students do not have to understand the set of sentences to respond correctly; in fact, they need only locate the subject of each sentence and conjugate the verb to respond. The meaning of the sentences is superfluous.

The next set of test items corresponds to the upper right quadrant of the Hadley model: The stimulus material consists of isolated sentences, unrelated to each other, but students have considerable leeway in their responses.

Example 2. A set of divergent-response speaking items presented in isolated sentences

¿Cómo es tu vida? Listen as your teacher reads some questions aloud. After each one, you will have 15 seconds to record your spoken answer **en español**. Say as much as you can in the time allotted after each question.
    1. ¿Qué actividades hay para los estudiantes en tu escuela?
    2. ¿Qué haces con tus amigos en un fin de semana típico?
    3. ¿Cuál es tu programa de televisión favorito? ¿Por qué te gusta?

Although the title of the test section once again suggests a common context for the oral questions, the context is very broad.

From the perspective of the student, there is no way to predict what topic each question will address. Although students have considerable freedom in how they choose to respond to each question, they will probably lose valuable response time adjusting their frame of reference to a new topic after they hear each new question.

Hadley suggests that teachers use segments of naturalistic discourse as the stimulus material for their test activities. Let us see what a convergent listening test activity based on sequential discourse might look like. This test format corresponds to the lower left-hand quadrant of the Hadley model.

Example 3. A set of convergent-response listening items that test grammar in a naturalistic discourse context

Instructions. You will hear Adriana and Felipe talk about Adriana's frightening experience. The second time their conversation will have pauses. Fill in the blanks with the missing verbs in the preterite or the imperfect. Replay the tape as often as necessary.

Students see:

FELIPE: ¿Cuál hombre? Yo no (1) _____ a nadie.
            ¿De qué hablas?
ADRIANA: El hombre que (2) _____ hablando por
            teléfono.
FELIPE: Pues, no, no lo (3) _____.
ADRIANA: ¡Era el mismo hombre!
FELIPE: ¿El mismo? ¿El mismo qué?
ADRIANA: El mismo hombre de Sevilla, el que me (4) ____ hasta el
            hotel, el hombre del anillo raro.
FELIPE: ¿Estás segura, Adriana?
ADRIANA:Totalmente segura. Te lo juro, (5) ____ el mismo anillo.

Students hear:

FELIPE: ¿Cuál hombre? Yo no vi a nadie. ¿De qué hablas?
ADRIANA: El hombre que estaba hablando por teléfono.
FELIPE: Pues, no, no lo vi.
ADRIANA: ¡Era el mismo hombre!

FELIPE: ¿El mismo? ¿El mismo qué?
ADRIANA: El mismo hombre de Sevilla, el que me siguió hasta el
            hotel, el hombre del anillo raro.
FELIPE: ¿Estás segura, Adriana?
ADRIANA: Totalmente segura. Te lo juro, llevaba el mismo anillo.
                (Adapted from Renjilian-Burgy et al. 1999, pp. 101-102)

This listening test activity is considered convergent because each
blank can be filled with one and only one correct answer.
However, the context in which the activity is embedded is natural
discourse, which helps students to anticipate what will be needed
to fill in the gaps. The whole activity is more authentic and more
communicative than Examples 1 and 2, which are based on
isolated sentences.

Finally, let us look at an example of a test activity from the
lower right quadrant of the Hadley model. This test activity
follows the one above: Students listen to the conversation
between Felipe and Adriana for a third time (and may also refer
to the printed version that they have just completed) and respond
in writing to open-ended questions.

Example 4. A set of divergent-response items that test writing, listening, and reading skill in a naturalistic discourse context

Instructions. Listen again to the conversation between Felipe and
Adriana. Then write en español your responses to the questions below.

1. ¿Por qué tiene Adriana tanto miedo?
2. ¿Cómo reacciona Felipe a lo que Adriana le dice?
                (Adapted from Renjilian-Burgy et al. 1999, p. 102)

Hadley (2000) would characterize this test activity as having a
"mixed-skills format" (p. 414) because it combines listening,
reading, and writing skills. It also exploits the naturalistic
discourse context by asking students to understand the
conversation as a whole, not just small sections of it.

As the foregoing examples show, test formats that entail
divergent responses offer students opportunities to write or speak

at length, expressing meaning in personal or creative ways. Needless to say, these response formats are considerably more time-consuming to grade. Hadley suggests that we design test formats that strike a balance between the more communicative divergent response types and the more economical convergent response types, but that we consistently couch the formats in naturalistic discourse beyond the sentence level. She calls this a "hybrid approach" (p. 397) to classroom testing, and continues her discussion as follows:

> Such an approach combines the concern for assessing specific features of language with a focus on communicative language use in context. That is, tests can be constructed to integrate specific lexical, grammatical, sociolinguistic, and discourse features so that they are assessed *as they operate in naturalistic discourse contexts* throughout the test. This means that there is little place for single-sentence items on course exams or quizzes. Rather, language use must be tested beyond the level of the sentence.
>
> (Hadley 2000, p. 397; emphasis in the original)

This approach to classroom testing may seem daunting to teachers who have traditionally relied on the test banks that accompany their textbooks and who may believe that discrete test items presented in isolated sentences are the only way to evaluate students' linguistic knowledge in an economical fashion. We support a different perspective—that linguistic knowledge isolated from the surrounding communicative contexts is an impoverished and partial form of knowledge that should not be tested at all. This perspective may seem somewhat radical, but with practice it is not hard to create test activities that are quick and easy to correct (i.e., convergent response types) and yet present language in contexts beyond the sentence level.

Teachers may wonder whether it is difficult to test linguistic knowledge, particularly grammatical knowledge, in a communicative context. Experience will show that pushing students to integrate and synthesize their knowledge in communicatively oriented tests actually helps them understand the form-meaning connections that underlie the language acquisition process. Let us consider a communicative test format that takes as its starting point the decontextualized convergent-response format in Example 1 above.

Example 5. A set of convergent-response grammatical items presented in a communicative context

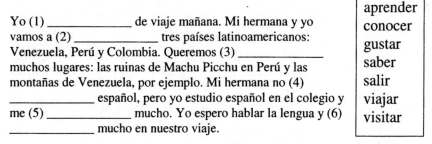

De viaje. Complete the following passage by choosing from the box at the right the verbs that make the most sense in the context. For some verbs you need to supply the appropriate form of the present indicative (e.g., **habla**). For others, the infinitive (e.g., **hablar**) is required. ¡**OJO!** The context is important, so read carefully. You may use each verb only once.

Yo (1) _____ de viaje mañana. Mi hermana y yo vamos a (2) _____ tres países latinoamericanos: Venezuela, Perú y Colombia. Queremos (3) _____ muchos lugares: las ruinas de Machu Picchu en Perú y las montañas de Venezuela, por ejemplo. Mi hermana no (4) _____ español, pero yo estudio español en el colegio y me (5) _____ mucho. Yo espero hablar la lengua y (6) _____ mucho en nuestro viaje.

| aprender |
| conocer |
| gustar |
| saber |
| salir |
| viajar |
| visitar |

One communicative feature of this set of test items is that students must comprehend the context to select the appropriate word for each blank. A second feature is that they must integrate their linguistic knowledge—present-indicative verb forms, function of the infinitive with a conjugated verb to indicate intention or future action, one instance of *gustar* along with the other verbs, and vocabulary—with their overall comprehension of the paragraph. Finally, the use of extended discourse allows the teacher to embed a test of linguistic knowledge into a culturally rich context in a natural way, thus reinforcing cultural concepts or information that may have already been presented in class.

For the teacher, this test format has the advantage of being quick and easy to grade, while at the same time reflecting the richness and complexity of communication in Spanish. Students may initially complain that this test format is too challenging because it combines topics that were presented separately in class or because they have to think about several aspects of the Spanish language at once. Once these communicatively rich formats become a regular part of the instructional culture, however, students will come to expect them and will adjust their expectations accordingly.

The foregoing discussion of test formats includes examples that touch on all language skills. In the sections below, we turn our attention to the evaluation of students' speaking ability. Although it is possible to imagine speaking test formats with convergent responses, most teachers would agree that this is not a desirable approach to evaluate students' oral skills. Instead, we should aim to evaluate students' speaking skills in divergent-response formats, where students have opportunities to express meaning, interact meaningfully with other students, and resolve expression and comprehension problems that may arise. How, then, do we test speaking in ways that are communicative, and yet not unduly burdensome in terms of administration and scoring time? We consider a range of formats for oral assessments and how they may be administered and scored economically and reliably.

FORMATS FOR COMMUNICATIVE ORAL ASSESSMENTS

If we agree with the principle that our speaking tests should mirror the goals and content of the speaking component of the curriculum, then we need to begin with a consideration of the types of speaking activities we use in our teaching. Here are some speaking activities that naturally occur in many Spanish classrooms.

- Students answer questions posed by the teacher, or the teacher may engage the class in conversation about such current topics as recently released films, a crime in the community, or vacation plans.

- Students interact in pairs to complete an activity presented by their teacher or found in their textbook. The activity may consist of a topic to discuss, questions to answer, or information to discover from each other. Students may later report to the class what they have learned from their partner or what conclusion they have reached in their discussion.
- Students in pairs or small groups prepare a skit or role play and perform it for the class.
- Students working individually or in pairs or small groups prepare a report to present to the class, and then give their presentation and respond to questions from their classmates.
- Students converse with each other in computer-mediated online chats. These interactions may be free conversations, or the teacher may pose topics for the students to discuss.
- Teachers may conduct oral interviews with students that are modeled on the ACTFL Oral Proficiency Interview (OPI).

Let us see how some of these activities can be transformed or adapted as oral test formats.

DESIGNING QUICK-AND-EASY ORAL ASSESSMENTS

If you had to choose a set of student behaviors or habits of work that, when implemented consistently over a period of time, contribute substantially to the development of speaking skills, what would you choose? We would cast our vote for an approach to the daily work of Spanish class that is enthusiastic, collaborative, and attentive. Volunteering to speak, taking advantage of pair and small-group activities to communicate as much as possible with one's classmates, and demonstrating effort and enthusiasm are behaviors that lead to improvements in fluency and confidence. How might we use oral tests to promote these behaviors in class?

USING CLASS ACTIVITIES AS ORAL ASSESSMENTS

One approach is to make every pair or small-group activity a scored evaluation activity for one pair or group of students. Over the course of a trimester or marking period, every student will be observed and evaluated during several of these activities. No modifications to the activities are needed; teachers need only develop a simple evaluation scale and use it regularly. We suggest that this scale incorporate verbal behaviors that, we believe, contribute to the development of oral skills. The sample scale in Figure 3 is intended for a pair activity. More columns could be added for group activites. The scale itself should be simply and easy to use. For example, for each criterion, 3 = always or almost always; 2 = sometimes; 1 = rarely or never.

**Figure 3. Sample evaluation scale for an informal
        oral assessment**

Observed behavior	Student #1	Student #2
Demonstrates enthusiasm and energy for the activity.		
Listens carefully to the partner; demonstrates interest in what the partner is saying.		
Asks the partner questions to clarify what partner says and to encourage expansion.		

We recommend sharing this evaluation scale with students, so that they know what is expected of them and what they can do to acquire the maximum number of points. A system like this one exploits the positive side of the washback effect, because it rewards students for doing things that we believe contribute to their learning. This type of oral assessment takes the teacher no time at all to administer, because it consists of the teacher observing a group of students doing something that they would be doing anyway, just as part of the class. Nor does it take any additional time to evaluate, because the teacher can easily score the students individually in their pairs or small groups while observing them.

EVALUATING STUDENTS ON ORAL ACTIVITIES CONDUCTED OUTSIDE OF CLASS

Another efficient strategy is to design an oral test that students take outside of class and record on audio tape. The teacher does have to listen to them to evaluate them, of course, although having them on tape gives the teacher flexibility about when and where to listen to them. The principal time-saving feature lies in not having the teacher administer them in class.

Example 6. Leave your teacher a message: An outside-of-class oral assessment

Instructions. Call your teacher on the phone and leave a message in Spanish on the voice mail or answering machine. [Administrative note: If possible, have students call a number dedicated to this purpose; e.g., a cell phone with voice mail, or a school number in the evening or over the weekend.] Your message should include the following information: your name, the day and time of your call, and the message you want to leave for your teacher. Leave a spontaneous message, just as you would in English. Do not write your message and then read or recite it from memory. You will lose points if your message does not sound spontaneous.

Evaluation. Your performance will be evaluated on its comprehensibility, inclusion of the three pieces of information requested, and spontaneity.

Descriptor	Points
Message sounds spontaneous, is fully comprehensible, and includes all three elements.	10

115

Message sounds spontaneous, is too brief and/or it is not completely comprehensible.	5
Message sounds as though it is being read or recited from memory (regardless of the completeness and comprehensibility of the content).	3
Student did not make the call, or made the call and did not leave a message.	0

(Adapted from Liskin-Gasparro 1996, p. 186)

Notice here that the evaluation scale is drawn from the features of a successful voice mail message in the real world: The person who receives the message knows who called, when the call came in, and why the person was calling. The scale is weighted to penalize students who try to circumvent the system by writing their message and then reading it aloud. The scale also subsumes grammatical and lexical accuracy under the general criterion of comprehensibility: If errors do not impede comprehensibility, students do not lose points for them in this assessment.

In practice, the test activity is quick and easy to score. Each message lasts about 30 seconds, so a teacher could listen to 10 messages per day in under 10 minutes. For students, it represents the opportunity to carry out in Spanish a communicative activity that is second nature to them in their native language.

DESIGNING MULTI-STAGE OR EXTENSIVE ORAL ASSESSMENTS

The foregoing section discusses in generic terms how to convert oral class activity into an graded speaking assessment by evaluating student performance on a simple scale that rewards primarily active participation in the activity. We also present an example of an oral assessment that students perform outside of class, thus representing no sacrifice of class time by the teacher. Both examples have the benefit of being easy and quick to score.

In the paragraphs below, we discuss more elaborate versions of the same two types of activities: an oral evaluation based on a textbook activity and a speaking activity carried out by students outside of class. Following the two examples, we discuss how to develop a scoring rubric to evaluate student performance on these and other assessment activities.

CONVERTING TEXTBOOK ACTIVITIES INTO MULTISTAGE EVALUATION INSTRUMENTS

Most textbooks include activities that are intended to be carried out by students working in pairs and small groups. Many of these activities contain visual material and helpful guidelines for managing student-to-student interactions. Some of them, like the activity below, can be expanded into multistage activities for either teaching or testing. As we have discussed in earlier chapters, however, suggestions for meaningful follow-up activities are seldom included. To make oral evaluation activities truly communicative, there needs to be a purpose for the interaction and a way to make use of whatever information or perspectives students gather from communicating with each other.

The speaking test below has been adapted from an activity in a first-year college Spanish text. It deals with living arrangements and is carried out in two stages. In the first stage, students interview each other to see if their living patterns and preferences will make them compatible as roommates. In the second stage, they select as their "roommate" one of their two partners and explain to the class the reasons for the choice. The activity involves some creativity—students have to write at least two questions of their own, in addition to using the ones printed for them—and may involve some negotiation of meaning if communication breaks down. Notice how the activity is structured and sequenced to help students stay on task and how the information gathered in the first phase has to be analyzed and synthesized for use in the second phase.

Example 7. A speaking test activity for a group of 4 students

¿Quiénes son más compatibles? Imagínate que buscas un(a)
compañero(a) de cuarto para vivir contigo en la residencia (*dorm*) de la
universidad. En cada grupo de 4 personas, hay que decidir cómo crear
las dos parejas más compatibles. En la etapa 1, cada persona entrevista
a otra persona del grupo sobre sus preferencias y gustos. Puedes usar
estas preguntas, pero también necesitas escribir 2 preguntas originales.

Etapa 1: Entrevistas entre los (las) compañeros(as).

Preguntas	Persona #1	Persona #2	Persona #3	Persona #4
1. ¿A qué hora te levantas por la mañana?				
2. ¿A qué hora prefieres acostarte?				
3. ¿Qué tipo de música te gusta?				
4. ¿Escuchas música mientras estudias?				
5. ¿Eres una persona ordenada (*neat*) o desordenada (*messy*)?				
6. [tu pregunta]				
7. [tu pregunta]				

Etapa 2: La decisión. Ahora expliquen a la clase quiénes van
a vivir juntos(as) y por qué.
(Adapted from Marinelli and Mujica Laughlin 1998, p. 181)

Numerous variations on this activity are possible. To
provide fuller context for the activity, particularly with students

who have not yet lived away from home, the teacher could design a warm-up activity to elicit students' preferences in music, whether they feel more energetic in the morning or at night, and the like. The teacher might guide the class in generating additional questions, from which each group or individual could select for the additional questions. It would also be advisable for the teacher to provide students with some guidelines for the second phase of the activity: the amount of information expected, how to structure it, and the importance of both members of the pair participating equally in the report to the class.

DESIGNING A CONVERSATIONAL ACTIVITY TO BE COMPLETED OUTSIDE OF CLASS

If your school has a media lab or a supervised area in the library where a pair of students can tape a conversation, you may want to have students carry out a role play during a study hall or free period and record it on audio tape. These role plays may take some time to design, but they can be revised to incorporate the contexts and structures of more advanced levels and reused with students in successive years. You may also need to enlist the cooperation of a media or library aide to administer the tests to students. The following oral test was developed for Spanish language students at the college level, but the topics have been revised to make it more suitable for high school students.

Example 8. Meeting an old friend: A role play performed and recorded outside of class

Instructions. (Students receive these instructions when they arrive for the assessment.) Imagine that you and your partner are old friends who have not seen each other since one of you moved away 3 years ago. You are happy to see each other again, and have lots to talk about. In your conversation, you should touch on the following topics:

1. where you live now, and what the town is like (suggestion: pick a place that you know relatively well, and pretend that you have moved there so you have information to share)
2. your current activities—job, hobbies or sports, etc.
3. your plans after graduation
4. To end the conversation, one of you invites the other to do something the following day—a meal, a movie, shopping, etc. You should discuss the details of time, place, and activity before you say good-bye.

Evaluation. Remember that your performance will be evaluated on the following criteria:

- effort and enthusiasm to communicate (double weight)
- comprehensibility to each other (and to the teacher)
- grammatical accuracy
- range and accuracy of vocabulary
- coverage of topics listed above
- exclusive use of Spanish during the conversation

Administration notes to students. You may spend no more than 10 minutes in preparation before you begin. You and your partner may plan your conversation in either English or Spanish, but your preparation must be exclusively oral. You may not write down notes or consult books or notes during the preparation or the conversation. Before you begin, check that the recording equipment is working properly and that your voices are audible. Once you start the tape and begin your conversation, you may not stop the tape or start over. Whatever trouble you may have expressing yourself or understanding your partner, just do the best you can to continue the conversation. When you are finished, rewind the tape, write both of your names on it, and return it and this instruction sheet to the monitor.

(Liskin-Gasparro 1988)

The resulting taped conversations may last from 5 to 15 minutes in length, depending on the students' proficiency level and the number and types of topics included in the role play. We have detailed above sample criteria for evaluation, which can be determined according to the teacher's priorities. In any case, we recommend that the evaluation criteria be shared with students well ahead of time.

In assigning students to pairs for an evaluation activity like this one, we recommend putting students with partners of comparable ability so that they are not intimidated or overpowered by a stronger partner, or forced to assume responsibility for the whole conversational task if paired with a partner who has considerably weaker skills.

SCORING ORAL ASSESSMENTS

There are many factors to take into account in designing an evaluation system for oral assessments. As discussed earlier in this chapter, we advocate using assessments so that they support the teacher's instructional goals. For example, if you have placed priority in a course on integrating cultural products and perspectives into all content areas of the curriculum, then surely you will want to design an evaluation scale for your oral assessments that rewards students whose performance includes substantive cultural information. It is also essential to set realistic standards for accuracy, particularly grammatical accuracy. It may not be appropriate to expect error-free language or native-like performance from students at any level of instruction. Instead, teachers should think carefully about how to describe a performance at the top of the evaluation scale: How accurate does a student performance have to be to merit the top score?

The evaluation scales presented earlier in this chapter (e.g., Figure 3, Example 6) represent two approaches to evaluation. Figure 3 represents a simplified version of an analytic scale. Three aspects of student performance (enthusiasm and energy, demonstrated attention and interest, and interactivity in the form of questions) are scored individually. The score values (3, 2, 1) are defined in terms of the frequency with which the behaviors occur. It is important to note here that the linguistic aspects commonly evaluated in oral assessments—grammatical accuracy, range and appropriateness of vocabulary, fluency—are not included in this evaluation system. Instead, the emphasis is on student behaviors that contribute to successful group and small-group oral activities. The rationale is to encourage a positive washback effect of testing on teaching and learning by rewarding students for active participation in the interactions that lie at the heart of communicative language teaching. The simplicity of the evaluation system responds to the practical need for the teacher to assume both assessment and teaching roles at the same time. A more involved system might interfere with the teacher's instructional function and, in the case of evaluating student performance on commonplace oral activities, might be excessive.

In Example 6, the evaluation of each student's performance is determined by using a holistic scale. Each score level includes brief descriptions of all of the factors expected to occur together: spontaneity, comprehensibility, and completeness. The choice of factors to be included in a holistic scale is up to the individual teacher. In the case of Example 6, the factors are drawn from the characteristics of a successful voice mail message. The commonly assessed linguistic factors (e.g., grammar, vocabulary) are included indirectly as they affect comprehensibility and, perhaps, completeness, but in this assessment activity linguistic accuracy does not play a role independent of its communicative function.

Analytic and holistic scoring rubrics present challenges to both designers and users. In designing any kind of scoring rubric, the first and most important decision is which factors of the performance to include in the evaluation system and which to leave out. This decision is based on the teacher's goals and priorities in general, and for the assessment in particular. Practical considerations also are important, such as the time available for scoring the assessment and the weight that a particular assessment has in the grading system as a whole.

The second decision is how to word the descriptions at each of the score points. Inevitably, the first draft of the rubric includes wording based on experience and expectations, not on evidence from actual student performances. The best rubrics take into account sample performances; if time permits, teachers may decide to do a kind of informal field test of the rubric. What does this entail? First, the teacher selects a small sample of performances (perhaps six in total) that, based on her experience with the students, reflect strong, average, and weak oral skills in the class as a whole. Then she evaluates the performances using the rubric. Even given a small sample of performances, the teacher will be able to make adjustments to the scoring rubric, as well as add details that appear to be characteristic of each score point. It is particularly important to include the performances of strong students in the class, to get a realistic sense of what the top of the scale sounds like. When spontaneity is a requirement of the performance, even strong students will find themselves unable to call forth all of their knowledge and will instead rely on those aspects of the language that they can use automatically and comfortably. Once the rubric has been revised, the teacher should score the entire set (including the samples).

All scoring scales have both strengths and weaknesses. Holistic scoring emphasizes what students do well. For teachers who have a tendency to focus primarily on accuracy, the descriptions in a holistic scale serve as a constant reminder of the role of grammar to support communication. However, the holistic descriptions of performance at each score level may not represent well the performances of students that do not match any of the descriptors. Another challenge for users of holistic scales is to constantly monitor themselves to make sure that they are taking all parts of a score level description equally seriously, and not reducing the evaluation to one or two aspects of the performance while ignoring the others (Cohen 1994, p. 315).

Analytic scoring may appear to be more objective than the use of a holistic scale, because it allows users to consider in isolation factors such as fluency, active participation, and grammatical accuracy. In fact, it is easier to train a group of teachers to evaluate performances reliably with an analytic scale (Cohen 1994, p. 317). However, in practice analytic scoring may be less objective than it appears on the surface, because it may not always be possible to consider factors in a speaking performance independently of each other. In addition, since the evaluation is conducted in stages (one scale at a time), teachers may unconsciously allow the first score to influence subsequent ones (Cohen 1994, p. 317).

Ultimately, the system that may be fairest to students is one that uses different types of rubrics during a semester or marking period. This variety minimizes the disadvantages of each system and takes advantages of its strengths. Let us see how student performance in the conversational task in Example 8 above could be scored by a teacher while listening to the conversations taped by each pair of students.

DESIGNING AN ANALYTIC SCORING SYSTEM FOR A CONVERSATIONAL TASK

To evaluate the performance of two students who are engaged in a collaborative task, we recommend designing a form that enables the teacher to take notes while listening to a live or taped performance, and then to record the scores for both students for each factor included in the assessment, all on a single piece of paper. A speaking activity similar to the one in Example 8 is comprehensive in nature, calling forth students' overall conversational ability. For this reason, students are assessed according to six aspects of their oral performance, shown in Figure 4. Given the time that the teacher invests in evaluating the performances, this type of assessment cannot be given frequently. It is possible, of course, to reduce the number of factors or use different ones, depending on the nature and purpose of the assessment.

Figure 4. Oral assessment scoring sheet for a pair or group performance

Student: _____ Score: _____	Student: _____ Score: _____

EFFORT/AMOUNT:
   8 6   4   2
	EFFORT/AMOUNT:
	   8 6 4 2

COMPREHENSIBILITY:
   4 3   2   1
	COMPREHENSIBILITY:
	   4 3 2 1

GRAMMATICAL ACCURACY:
   4 3   2   1
	GRAMMATICAL ACCURACY:
	   4 3 2 1

VOCABULARY:
   4 3   2   1
	VOCABULARY:
	   4 3 2 1

COVERAGE OF TOPICS:
   6 3   2   1   0
	COVERAGE OF TOPICS:
	   6 3 2 1 0

EXCLUSIVE USE OF SPANISH:
   4 3   2   1
	EXCLUSIVE USE OF SPANISH:
	   4 3 2 1

After deciding which factors to include in the assessment, the teacher must create descriptors for each scale. If this were a proficiency assessment (which it is not), the performance of each student would be evaluated according to a scale in which the descriptors for each score point would be the same, no matter who was being assessed. This is the case with the ACTFL Oral Proficiency Interview, for example; the criteria for a rating of Novice High or Intermediate Mid are always the same, regardless of how long an individual has studied the language. In most classroom assessments, it makes sense to link our evaluative judgments to our expectations for students at a particular course level or even in a particular class.

To design a scoring scale, we start first with a generic scale, which we then adapt to each of the evaluative criteria.

Figure 5. Generic scale

4	Excellent
3	Very good or good
2	Not so good; weak
1	Very poor

We prefer a scale with an even number of score points (4 rather than 5, for instance) because of the temptation to assign a disproportionate number of scores at the midpoint that is permitted by a scale with an odd number of score points. A scale with an even number of score points forces the teacher to listen more carefully and to make more reasoned evaluative judgments. In the case of a 4-point scale, scores of 4 and 3 are reserved for performances in the upper half of the group, whereas scores of 2 and 1 are for performances in the lower half. If you have a particularly strong or particularly weak class, you may want to adjust your relative proportions of high and low scores. You may decide to apply a curve to the final (total) scores of your group at the end of the process if you find that you have been more severe or more lenient than the overall performance of your students merits.

We like to give extra weight to elements of the speaking performance that we believe will enhance the value of the activity as a learning opportunity, as well as contribute to students' confidence overall. We most often privilege the criterion "effort and enthusiasm to communicate" in this way, because demonstrated interest in what the partner is saying and energetic participation in the activity creates a positive tone for the activity, contributes to learning, and is something that students at all ability levels can control. The score scale for this criterion might look something like Figure 6:

Figure 6. 4-point scale for effort and enthusiasm to communicate

4	Makes zealous efforts to communicate; uses many verbal resources; shows great interest in partner's contribution
3	Manifests considerable energy and enthusiasm
2	Uses generic phrases; just goes through the motions
1	Not interactive

In evaluating students' grammatical accuracy in a spontaneous speaking activity, it is important to establish realistic standards for an excellent or very good performance. The scale for "grammatical accuracy" in Figure 7 takes into account students' knowledge level and the performance errors that are a natural part of spontaneous speech.

Figure 7. 4-point scale for grammatical accuracy

4	All or most utterances are substantially correct. Minor errors (e.g., agreement) occur randomly, not consistently. Errors in structures that are new or unknown to students should be ignored.
3	Many utterances are substantially correct, but shows some problems with structures that have been extensively used in class.
2	Speech characterized by many inaccuracies. Only about half of the utterances are substantially accurate.
1	Very few accurate utterances.

The procedure for creating the scoring rubrics for the remaining criteria is the same. We have taken a quantitative approach in the scoring of the criterion of topic coverage: 3 points for the invitation sequence, and 1 point each for the other topics.

INTERVIEW PROCEDURES AS ORAL ASSESSMENTS

The interview is a time-honored format for the assessment of students' speaking skills. We are reluctant to recommend interviews conducted by the teacher with individual students because of the time involved not only for the interviews themselves, but also the instructional time that is lost while the teacher is conducting the interviews. In addition, students may find the one-on-one interview with the teacher intimidating. Research on language interview tests (Perrett 1990, Young and Milanovic 1992) has found, unsurprisingly, that it is the interviewer who asks most of the questions, chooses the topics, and controls the turn-taking procedures.

The ACTFL oral proficiency interview (OPI) may be the language interview test with which teachers are most familiar. Based on a proficiency scale and interview procedure developed for use with U.S. State Department employees, the ACTFL OPI has been administered to high school and college students since the early 1980s. Two decades of experience with the OPI have demonstrated that it is most fruitfully used to measure major changes in speaking ability that occur over a long period of time (e.g., by the end of a multiyear sequence of language study) or after a significant linguistic experience (e.g., several weeks or months living and studying abroad). Information on the OPI and the proficiency scale on which interviewee performance is rated can be found in many publications, including Hadley (2000) and the ACTFL web page (http://www.actfl.org).

Two language proficiency interview tests based on the ACTFL OPI have made the procedure more accessible to high school students and their teachers. The modified oral proficiency interview (MOPI), which measures speaking ability at the Novice and Intermediate levels, has made oral proficiency testing (including tester certification through ACTFL) a viable professional activity for those whose own speaking ability is at the Advanced level. Indirect speaking tests, often referred to as simulated oral proficiency interviews (SOPIs) are more efficient to use than direct, face-to-face interview tests. A SOPI can be administered to individual students or, preferably, to a group of students in a media lab setting: Instructions are given by a master tape, and students record their responses on individual audio cassettes. The Center for Applied Linguistics (CAL) has developed SOPIs in a number of languages, including Spanish and Portuguese. A self-instructional rater training kit is available in Spanish. Information about SOPIs can be found on the CAL web site (http://www.cal.org/tests/fltests.html).

The Center for Advanced Research on Language Acquisition (CARLA) at the University of Minnesota has developed the Contextualized Speaking Assessment (CoSA), a type of SOPI that takes 20 minutes to administer and is designed to assess whether students can speak at a particular level on the ACTFL proficiency scale. One task from a sample Intermediate-level CoSA is displayed on the CARLA web page (http://carla.acad.umn.edu/CoSA.html). The Spanish version of the task is presented here as a model that teachers can use to develop similar assessment activities for their own students.

Example 9. A sample task from the University of Minnesota contextualized speaking assessment (CoSA)

Theme: The New Exchange Student

It is the first week of school, and when you walk into class, you see the new exchange student sitting by herself. You introduce yourself to Cristina, who says that she is from Lima, and that she has just arrived in the United States. You have been studying Spanish, and you would like to make her feel welcome.

Segment 1

Cristina wonders about you: where you're from, how old you are, what you're studying, and so on. Wait until you hear Cristina speak, then tell her about yourself.

15 second pause for student to think about what to say, then student hears, but does not see, a prompt:

"Y tú, cuéntame de ti."

Student then has 60 seconds in which to respond.

Sample student response to Segment 1 (corrections are indicated in italics)

Soy de Cleveland Ohio. Tengo veinte años. Mi especialización es las Ciencias Políticas. Durante el fin de semana, me gusta juego con mi ni-, hijo. También me gusta correr muchas milas *(millas)*. También me gusta todos mis clases. Y . . . me gusta esquilar *(escalar)* los montañas y además nedo *(nado)* en el lago.

Segment 2

You would like to learn more about Cristina and her life in Lima: her family, friends, interests, and studies. Wait until you hear Cristina ask a question, then ask her at least five questions to find out more about her life in her country.

15 second pause for student to think about what to say, then student hears, but does not see, a prompt:

"Ya nos hemos hablado mucho. Y tú, ¿qué quieres saber de mí?

Student then has 60 seconds in which to respond.

(http://carla.acad.umn.edu/CoSA-sample.html)

SUMMARY

In this chapter we began by reviewing the roles that testing can play in a Spanish program—to place students into courses, to assign grades, to motivate students. To these functions we could add that of self-assessment or program assessment for teachers. Tests can help us analyze the effectiveness of our teaching on a particular topic, or can give us information on the development of students' communicative ability. Sometimes it is only through communicative assessments that we see how students perform when they are speaking independently, outside the restricted realm of language practice.

In the second part of the chapter we introduced Hadley's model of testing formats and showed, through examples, how even convergent (one and only one correct answer) response formats can be couched in naturalistic language to increase their communicative value. In the final section of the chapter we presented several examples of oral assessments, along with guidelines on how student performances might be evaluated.

We conclude by returning to the questions that opened the chapter.

Question 1: What kinds of oral tests should we give?

    a. Speaking assessments should be done one-on-one with the teacher so that each student's performance can be evaluated independently.

    b. Because real-world speaking usually occurs in pairs or groups, oral tests should also be given to pairs or groups of students together.

    c. We should plan to use a variety of oral assessments to reflect the speaking activities in the curriculum.

Question 2: How should student performances on oral interaction tests be evaluated?

    a. Because speaking is a complex activity that consists of many parts, a single holistic score is most appropriate.

    b. Objectivity should be the teacher's first priority in evaluation, so a system like counting errors to arrive at a score is most appropriate.

    c. Because evaluation is a part of instruction, a system for scoring oral interactions that fits the teacher's goals for the test is most appropriate.

We hope that you can see why we have indicated "c" as the best answer to both questions.

APPLICATION ACTIVITIES FOR REFLECTION AND DISCUSSION

1. Explain in your own words the concept of "washback" as it is used to characterize the influence of tests on student and teacher behavior and on the teaching/learning context. Give two examples of washback, one positive and one negative.
2. Select a course or level that you are currently teaching (e.g., Spanish 3 at the secondary level; Intermediate Spanish I at the college level). Respond to the following questions.
    a. What percentage of your students' grades are related to speaking?
    b. Does this percentage correspond to the emphasis that you give to oral activities in class, or to what you mentally give to the speaking skill?
    c. If the correspondence in b. is not what you would like it to be, what adjustments might you make?
3. Select a speaking activity from your textbook (or one that you have designed) that is typical of the types of speaking activities you frequently use. Following the suggestions in this chapter, convert it to a speaking evaluation by writing instructions to the students on how to proceed. In addition, design a quick and easy scoring scale for the activity. Explain your selection of the factors that you included in the scoring scale.
4. Should the instructions for students in a speaking evaluation be given in Spanish or in English? Explain the reasons for your response.
5. Following the model of the University of Minnesota CoSA sample task presented in this chapter, design a speaking task at the same level but based on a different theme.

CLASSROOM INTERACTION

Question 1: Please follow the instructions below.

First, read the two classroom interactions presented below.

Example A
Teacher: ¿Cómo te llamas?
Student: Alex
Teacher: ¿Alex?
Student: Sí,
Teacher: Mucho gusto, Alex.

Example B
Teacher: ¿Cómo te llamas
Student: Nick.
Teacher: Me llamo Nick.
Student: Me llamo Nick.
Teacher: Muy bien, Nick.

Now, relate each statement below to the example(s) to which it refers.
Example A = A   Example B = B   Examples A and B = A & B
 A, B, or A & B?
_____ a. The teacher is interested in learning the student's name.
_____ b. The teacher expects students to answer in complete sentences.
_____ c. What the student says is less important than how he says it.
_____ d. What the student says is more important than how he says it.
_____ e. The teacher rewards the student for correctly answering.
_____ f. The teacher responds to the student in a "real-life" manner.

Question 2: Please choose the most appropriate response.
  How the teacher structures and uses Spanish in the classroom
  ___.

  a. informs students what behaviors the teacher considers acceptable
  b. affects the way students use Spanish
  c. suggests to students how Spanish is used outside the classroom
  d. All of the statements are correct.

INTRODUCTION

"We now know that learners learn a language best when they are provided opportunities to use the target language to communicate in a wide range of activities. The more learners use the target language in meaningful situations, the more rapidly they achieve competency."
(National Standards in Foreign Language Education Project 1996, p. 37)

The development of students' language proficiency is the primary goal of the communicative classroom. In Chapter 3 we discuss the communicative classroom, including approaches to instructional design that include task-based instruction and learning scenarios modeled on the *Standards*. We assert that these approaches to language instruction provide numerous contexts in which students can use Spanish and by so doing, increase their Spanish language proficiency. We argue that teachers should teach (almost!) exclusively in Spanish, in part because if teachers want their students to speak Spanish, they need to speak Spanish themselves. What we merely alluded to, however, is the importance of the way language is used by teachers and students in the classroom.

In this chapter, we briefly describe language used in "real life," or outside the classroom. We also discuss sample classroom interaction practices, including snippets of actual classroom discourse from ESL and foreign language classrooms. By analyzing and reflecting on these practices, we identify things teachers can do to promote optimal student participation and language development.

CAREGIVER TALK, FOREIGNER TALK, AND TEACHER TALK

Imagine the following situation. You are the proud parent of a small child you've just picked up from preschool. Read over the two snippets provided below. How would you respond to the child's last statement--as in Example A or Example B?

Example A
Parent: How was school today?
Child: It was fun.
Parent: What was fun about it?
Child: A clown comed to our class.
Parent: A clown? What'd he do?

Example B
Parent: How was school today?
Child: It was fun.
Parent: What was fun about it?
Child: A clown comed to our class.
Parent: A clown **came** to your class. It's not **comed**; it's **came.**

Although we sometimes correct as in Example B, more often than not we choose to listen to the child and encourage him or her to say more as in Example A. "Caregiver talk" is defined as the language used by parents or caregivers when interacting with children. It is characterized by speech modifications intended to make language more comprehensible to children (e.g., slower rate of speech, stressing key words, repeating). Similarly, "foreigner talk," the language used by native speakers when addressing non-native speakers in non-classroom situations, is marked by adjustments similar to those of caregiver talk:

(NS = Native Speaker)
NS: You're not working right now?
Rafaela: No.
NS: No?
Rafaela: Ahh...for one week...I...the...comp-any? The company...is inventory...inventory. Aha, for one week.
NS: Oh.

Rafaela: Monday I work. I work...Monday.
NS: You're going to start working Monday again.
                   (Adapted from Hatch 1978, pp. 425-426)

Lightbown and Spada note: "Error correction...tends to be limited to corrections of meaning--including errors in vocabulary choice--in first language acquisition [child language].   In informal second language acquisition, errors which do not interfere with meaning are usually overlooked...Errors of grammar and pronunciation are rarely remarked on, but the wrong word choice may receive comment from a puzzled interlocutor" (p. 22). As in Example A and in the example of foreigner talk, research has shown that users of caregiver and foreigner talk, when interacting with children and non-native speakers, respectively, respond more to a child's or non-native speaker's message than to the message's form. In other words, in the "real-world" outside the classroom, people tend to pay more attention to **what** a first (or second) language child or non-native speaker says, and less to **how** he or she says it (e.g., Lightbown and Spada 1993).

"Teacher talk" is the language typically used by teachers in the foreign language classroom. Like caregiver or foreigner talk, teacher talk is also characterized by adjustments (e.g., repetitions, rephrasing, emphasis) to make the second or foreign language comprehensible to learners. Yet though many teachers make such modifications when, say, presenting vocabulary (see Chapter 3 on Presenting Vocabulary [Comprehensible Input]), they oftentimes do not do so during routine classroom interaction. In other words, the same teacher who is careful about how he "inputs" car vocabulary (e.g., *Estos objetos se llaman* ***llantas o neumáticos***. *Las **llantas** o los **neumáticos** son redondos y negros, y es necesario tener cuatro*), may be the same teacher who structures his language in a manner that does not encourage students to "share" and to use their Spanish more freely.

Studies on classroom interaction on non-second/foreign language classrooms (e.g., Mehan 1979; Sinclair and Coulthard

1975), as well as research on second and foreign language classes (e.g., Brooks 1990, 1993; Chaudron 1988; Hall 1995) suggest that most teacher talk and interaction practices do not encourage optimal student interaction. Unlike caregiver or foreigner talk that focuses more on *what* is said, teacher talk focuses more on *how* something is said. As illustrated in Figure 1, a common pattern of classroom interaction is initiation > response > evaluation (feedback). In this interaction pattern the teacher asks a question of one or more students (I), the student or students reply (R), and the teacher evaluates or gives feedback (E) on the appropriateness of the student response. Brooks (1992) has referred to this as a ping-pong game of questions and answers.

Figure 1: Common Classroom Interaction Pattern

I $\rightarrow$	**R** $\rightarrow$	**E**
Initiation	**Response**	**Evaluation/Feedback**
(By Teacher)	(By One or More Students)	(By Teacher)

The following example is from Brooks (1990). During a form-focused exercise on practicing adjective opposites, the follow interaction took place:

> *(T = Teacher; C = Class)*
> T: ¿Okay? Bien. ¿Cuál es el opuesto de bonita?
> C: Fea.
> T: Fea. Muy bien. *(indicating approval)*
>   Bonita. Fea. *(repetition/reinforcement of pair)*
>   Bien. *(closes interactional unit)*
>   ...
>   Gorda.
> C: Flaca.
> T: Flaca. Bien. *(closes interactional unit)* (p. 163)

In this example we see how the teacher initiates (*¿Cuál es el opuesto de bonita?* and later *Gorda*); students then reply (*fea; flaca*); and then the teacher gives feedback (*Muy bien* or *Bien*).

Although it could be said that the use of I > R >E is understandable given the narrow focus of the goal of the exercise (to practice adjectives), this interaction pattern is the most commonly used, even for "open-ended" (i.e., non-linguistic focused) interactions. In other words, even when teachers expect students to "share" information about themselves in Spanish (e.g., *¿Qué hiciste este fin de semana?*) or to express their opinions (e.g., *¿Estás a favor o en contra de la pena de muerte?*), they are likely to organize classroom discourse in the I > R > E pattern. As this pattern is the most common found in classrooms, it is important to examine the teacher talk used in interactions, particularly during the "E" (evaluation/feedback) phase.

Although Spanish is more a second than a "foreign" language in the United States, for many students the Spanish classroom may nonetheless afford them their only opportunity to develop their communicative competence. As stated in the quote from the *Standards* at the beginning of this section, we need to make sure we provide ample opportunities for language development to occur. And the way we speak—our "teacher talk"—as well as the way we structure our interaction, have a major impact on the extent to which our students develop their Spanish.

SAMPLE CLASSROOM INTERACTION PRACTICES

In the section that follows we discuss issues surrounding class discussions, question types, activity purpose, and communication behaviors. Throughout the discussion we provide examples of actual classroom discourse from ESL and foreign language classrooms, and suggest ways for teachers to provide optimal opportunities for their students to develop their communicative competence.

CLASS DISCUSSIONS

When we think of "ideal" class discussions, we probably picture a lively interaction on a given topic in which most (if not all) students participate, each person directing what he or she says to everyone in the class--to fellow classmates as well as to the teacher. Below we will examine transcripts from Spanish classes from a discussion question format, as well as from a task-based format, and identify which comes closer to the "ideal" class discussion just described.

Discussion Questions

The following sample classroom interaction took place in a third-semester Spanish class. It fits the category of discussion questions because a question is posited which the teacher hopes most of the students will answer. This "warm-up" activity resembles the beginning of many Monday language classes in that that teacher wants to find out what students did over the weekend.

Scenario A (T = Teacher; Ss = Several students)

T: ¿Y qué pasó este fin de semana? Este fin de semana pasado

Jason: ¡Quiz mañana!

T: No, no, no. Yo sé que hay un quiz mañana. ¿Qué pasó...

Ss: Halloween. Fue Halloween.

Jason: Y un juego...no ganaron...no partido este

T: ¿Y era aquí el juego o en otra parte?

Jason: No, Purdue..fue mal.

T: OK, ¿y entonces para Halloween Uds. se disfrazaron?¿Se pusieron ropa?

Ss: Sí sí.

T: ¿Y de qué?

Adam: De una persona muy, muy gorda...

T: ¿Y cómo, cómo...?   *(Class laughs)* ¿Muy
         gordo? ¿Y cómo te hiciste gordo?
Adam: *¿Pillow?* ¿Cómo se dice *pillow?*
T: Una almohada.
Adam: *Pillow*, sí...
T: ¿Y fuiste a una fiesta?
Mandy: ¡A mi fiesta!
Adam: De Mandy.
T: Ah, Mandy, ¿tuviste una fiesta este fin de
         semana?
Mandy: Sí.
T: ¿Y cuántas personas fueron a la fiesta?
Mandy: No sé. Muchas personas.
T: ¿Y te disfrazaste también?
Mandy: Sí.
T: ¿De qué?
Mandy: De Cinderella.
T: ¿Y cómo cómo hiciste el traje de Cinderella?
         ¿Con qué?
Mandy: Un vestido muy blanco
T: ¿Largo? ¿Un vestido largo? *(Here teacher
         misinterpreted "largo" for "blanco")*
Mandy: Huh?
T: ¿Un vestido largo?
Mandy: Sí, un vestido largo. ¿Y cómo se dice "crown?"
T: Una corona.
Mandy: Sí, corona.
T: ¿Otras personas fueron a la fiesta de Mandy?
Ss: No no...
T: ¿No los invitaron? *(Laughter)* ¿Y quién más se
         disfrazó?

*(The interaction continues between the teacher and three
different students.)*
         (Unpublished data collected by Liskin-Gasparro 1998)

The teacher begins the class by asking students what happened
this weekend, with one student (Jason) attempting to change the

subject by mentioning tomorrow's quiz. The teacher responds to what Jason says (*No, no, no...Yo sé que hay un quiz mañana*), and redirects the class to her original question (*¿Qué pasó...*), with several students mentioning that it had been Halloween. Jason brings up the game *(Y un juego...no ganaron...no partido este..)*, the teacher asks him a related question, *¿Y era aquí el juego o en otra parte?*, he responds, and then the teacher focuses the discussion on the topic of Halloween in which students in the class had expressed interest (*OK, ¿y entonces para Halloween Uds. se disfrazaron? ¿Se pusieron ropa?*). Throughout her interactions with students, the teacher listens to what students say. Even at the beginning of class when Jason brings up an unrelated issue (tomorrow's quiz), and the fact that the school lost the game, the teacher listens to and responds to what he says. Sensing the majority of the students' interest in the topic of Halloween, she quickly establishes it as the topic of class discussion, and asks students questions related to that topic. She shows interest in what students say (*Ah, Mandy, ¿tuviste una fiesta este fin de semana?*), by asking related follow-up questions (*¿Y cuántas personas fueron a la fiesta?*), thus encouraging them to provide more information about their Halloween. When students need to use a vocabulary word for which they do not know the Spanish, they seek help by asking *¿Cómo se dice...?* And to the teacher and her students' credit, all of this is done in Spanish.

The only negative about this class discussion is that the interaction takes place between the teacher and several individual students. In the scenario above, a total of five students were willing to talk one-on-one with their teacher. Yet in many classrooms, even fewer students are willing to participate in such teacher-student discussions. It could be argued that this activity would elicit more student participation if it followed a task-based approach (e.g., The teacher could first ask students to interview a partner and write down two things he or she did for Halloween, followed then by a class discussion).

One Interesting Study: Discussion Questions vs. Task-Based Activity

Lee (2000) reports a study intended to compare, in part, the amount of student participation demonstrated during a discussion questions activity and during a task-based activity. Four third-semester Spanish classes participated, with two classes engaging in discussion questions, the other two in the task-based activity. The four class sessions were "guest taught" by the teacher-researcher. The content of the lessons was kept as similar as possible, with students asked to make associations about bilingualism and biculturalism and to suggest ways to becoming bilingual and bicultural. The lesson plans for the discussion questions and for the task-based activity groups were divided into several segments. Our discussion focuses on the first phase of each of these lessons. (The complete lesson plans for the Discussion Questions and the Task-Based Activity groups are provided in Appendix A.)

The **Discussion Questions** groups were asked two questions: *¿Qué asocian Uds. con el término bilingüe?* and *¿Qué asocian con el término bicultural?* A portion of one classroom transcript is provided below:

> **Scenario B - Discussion Questions** (T = Teacher-Researcher, Ss = several students, S1 =the first individual student to speak, S2 = the second individual student to speak; Italics denote English words used)
> T: Ahora quiero hablar con Uds. hoy sobre el bilingüismo. El bilingüismo. Uds.
>   todos estudian español. ¿Quieren ser bilingües? ¿Bilingües español-inglés?
> Ss: *(General murmuring of consent)*
> T: ¿Quién me puede decir lo que significa ser bilingüe? ¿Qué significa la
>   palabra? ¿Cuál es la definición de bilingüe?
> Ss: *(No answer. 5-second pause)*
> T: ¿Es una persona que habla una lengua?

Ss: No.

T: ¿Tres lenguas?

Ss: No, dos.

T: Dos. Dos. Es una persona que habla dos lenguas.
¿Cuándo yo digo la
palabra bilingüe, en qué piensan? De inmediato.
¿Qué asocian con el
término bilingüe?

Ss: *(No answer. 5-second pause)*

T: ¿Qué personas? ¿Qué cosas?

S1: Mi madre es bilingüe.

T: ¿Tu madre es bilingüe? ¿Qué idiomas habla?

S1: Inglés, español, *polish.*

T: Es trilingüe. ¿Es tu madre de ascendencia hispana?

S1: Sí.

T: ¿De qué país es?

S1: México.

T: ¿Es tu padre también bilingüe?

S1: No, papá Chicago.

T: Tu papá es de Chicago, pero hay muchos bilingües
en Chicago. ¡Muchísimos!

S1: Mi papá *Ireland.*

T: ¿Tu papá es de Irlanda? Yo lo soy, también. ¿Hay
otras personas en la clase que conocen a alguien
bilingüe?

S2: Mi mamá también es bilingüe.

T: ¿Sí? ¿Cuáles son las lenguas que habla?

...

*(The teacher continues to lead the class discussion on being
bilingual, and then on what students associate with being
bicultural. Only two students, S1 and S2, participated in the
interaction)*

(Adapted from Lee 2000, pp. 50; Original Spanish supplied by Lee)

Scenario B resembles Scenario A in that the teacher establishes
the topic of discussion, listens to what students say, and shows
interest in what they say by asking related follow-up questions.

144

Lee reports that at certain points during the discussion, murmuring could be heard and heads were seen nodding, but only two students volunteered to actively participate in the discussion.

For the first phase of the task-based lesson plan, the teacher-researcher divides students into groups of four and distributes a handout in which each student is asked to make a list of things he or she associates with being bilingual and with being bicultural. He tells the class: *"...Tienen que preparar dos listas. Tres minutos. Tienen tres minutos para hacer el Paso 1."* A portion of the transcript is provided below in Scenario C:

Scenario C -Task-Based Activity (T = Teacher-Researcher, G = Student who spoke on behalf of his/her small group; Italics denote English words used).

T: *[While students are working in small groups for three minutes, the teacher monitors the groups. Students ask him questions, especially about lexical items. The following interaction takes place after the three-minute group work.]*
   OK, vamos a ver. ¿Cuáles son las cosas que Uds. asocian primero con bilingüe, con este término. ¿Qué asocian Uds. con el término bilingüe? OK. Uds. una cosa, una cosa que tienen en la lista.

G1: Difícil.

T: Difícil. Es difícil ser bilingüe. OK. Y Uds. una cosa.

G2: Hablar más que una lengua.

T: Hablar más de una lengua. Ah jah. Es la definición. Otra cosa.

G3: Acentos y verbos diferentes.

T: Ah jah. Acentos y diferentes verbos. Muy bien. Este grupo.

G4: Inmigrante.

T: OK. ¿El inmigrante o los inmigrantes? OK. ¿Y aquí?

G5: Un mundano.

T: ¿Un qué?

G5: Un mundano, *worldly.*

T: OK. Alguien que conoce el mundo. Muy bien. Y aquí, este grupo.

G6: La profesor.

T: La profesora. OK. Es preferible que la profesora sea bilingüe para enseñarespañol. Sí. OK. Otra cosa en tu lista.

G6: ¿Bicultural?

T: No, bilingüe.

G6: Restaurantes.

T: Restaurantes bilingües. OK. *[Points to next group]*

G5: La inteligencia.

T: Inteligencia. ¿Otro? De este grupo.

G4: Embajadores.

T: Embajador. Es preferible que sean bilingües, pero no lo son en la realidad. *[Points to next group]*

G3: Lengua.

T: Lengua. ¿Qué más? ¿Tienen otra cosa?

G3: No.

T: ¿No? ¿No tienen otra cosa para añadir? OK. Y Uds. otra cosa.

G2: La inteligencia.

T: OK. ¿Cualquier grupo tiene algo en la lista que ya **no** se ha mencionado? ¿Tienen Uds. algo que no hemos mencionado hasta el momento?

G6: El doctor.

T: Un médico. Aja. Hay médicos bilingües. Otra cosa.

G3: El radio.

T: Sí, hay programas bilingües en el radio. ¿Algo más? Bicultural. Vamos a ver bicultural....

(The interaction continues on the topic of biculturalism.)
(Adapted from Lee 2000, pp. 53-54; Original Spanish provided by Lee)

In comparing this task-based activity of Scenario C with the discussion questions activity of Scenario B, we find that again the teacher listens to what students say, and responds to what they say by restating or asking related questions. What is interesting is that during the task-based activity, representatives from all six groups speak and tend to contribute multiple times. Whereas it could be argued that the teacher-researcher elicits more participation in Scenario C than in B because he calls on students (and does not do so in Scenario B), Lee reports (personal communication) that even students who did not contribute to the follow-up discussion reported in Scenario C did participate in the initial small-group activity and were more attentive overall. (In fact, the members of one group, not knowing the Spanish word for "worldly," wrote on the handout their own clever Spanish version, *mundano*.) Lee indicates: "The most dramatic contrast between this [task-based] transcript and the discussion is how much more content and information are elicited through the tasks" (p. 52). And in a follow-up recall test conducted one week later, students in the task-based activity classes remembered more information than students in the discussion questions classes.

In Chapter 3 we articulated the use of task-based instruction for lesson planning. The work of Lee and others as well as own experience lend support to the use of task-based activity, in that it is likely to promote greater learner participation and follow-up discussion. The positive elements of non- task-based Scenarios A and B as well as task-based Scenario C are that the teachers are interested in what students say, and they demonstrate their interest by asking related questions and by encouraging students to contribute more to the discussion, and that all this is done in Spanish. And even though the task-based activity shown in Scenario C does not fit the "ideal" classroom discussion described above (i.e., lively interaction in which all students participate, and do so by addressing all members of the class), it nonetheless provides for more student participation and information exchange.

Task-based activity design addresses a common concern of many language teachers, that of classroom management. In the discussion question scenarios A and B, the teacher maintains control by making sure that he or she is the focus of all interactions, i.e., the teacher asks questions, and individual students answer. Yet in most cases the teacher finds him-/herself "discussing" a topic with just a few individual students (who tend to be the better or the bolder students), with the rest of the class either paying attention or not. In the task-based scenario, the teacher's role changes. He or she serves as the architect--the person who designs the activity--and as the resource person to whom students can turn if they have questions (Lee and VanPatten, 1995). The teacher maintains control of the class in two ways: 1) through *a priori* design of the separate steps and 2) by careful management of time. Breaking open-ended questions (e.g.,¿*Se llega a ser bilingüe y bicultural de la misma manera?*) into steps helps to guide all students in generating ideas which they express in Spanish. While students work in groups on specific tasks, the teacher circulates through the room, answering students' questions students, and monitoring that they stay on-task. Having a specific task to carry out within a certain time limit encourages more students to participate, and to do so in a timely manner. The report-back or whole-class discussion portion of task-based lessons is then more structured and fruitful.

In sum, whole-class discussion questions are oftentimes used as warm-up activities (as in Scenario A), and they may arise spontaneously in response to student comments. Yet when the teacher wishes for greater student involvement and richer class discussions and can plan accordingly, it is recommended that he or she implement task-based activity design.

QUESTION TYPES

The types of questions teachers ask can affect the language that students produce in response. Our discussion focuses on two types of questions, display and referential.
Display questions, defined as questions whose answers are known to the person asking them, differ from "referential" questions. **Referential questions** seek new information that is unknown to the inquirer. Figure 1 presents sample display and non-display or referential questions typical of beginning level Spanish classrooms:

Figure 1: Sample Spanish Display and Referential Questions

Display	Non-Display or Referential
¿Qué día es hoy?	*¿Cuándo es tu cumpleaños?*
¿De qué color es tu camisa?	*¿Cuál es tu color favorito?*
¿Eres estudiante?	*¿Qué materias estudias?*
¿Dónde estás?	*¿Dónde te gusta correr?*

¿Qué día es hoy? is a display question because the teacher knows the answer, and wants a student to practice saying today's date. In contrast *¿Cuándo es tu cumpleaños?* is a referential question if the teacher does not know but wants to learn the student's birthday. Although display questions, including such types as *sí/no, cierto/falso*, either/or, and *¿Qué es esto?* have an important role for inputting or reviewing vocabulary, they are not the best choice for encouraging students to improve their speaking skills. Yet in a study carried out on teacher-learner interaction in elementary-level ESL classes, on average six of every seven questions asked by teachers were display (Long and Sato 1983).

The following exchange reported in Nunan (1987) takes place in a beginning-level ESL class. Immediately prior to the exchange, the teacher had asked students working in small groups to put a series of pictures in a logical order. You will note that all of the questions asked of students are of the display type.

Scenario D
T: What's the name of this? What's the name? Not in Chinese.
Ss: Van. Van.
T: Van. What's in the back of the van?
S: Milk. Milk.
T: Milk.
Ss: Milk. Milk.
T: A milk van.

S: Milk van.
T: What's this man? Driver.
S: Driver.
T: The driver.
S: The driver.

(Adapted from Nunan, pp. 142-143)

Following this exercise, the teacher decides to ask students to relate their own experiences to the picture sequence. The researcher noted that this was a departure for the teacher, whose language behaviors tended to be I > R > E with the "I" consisting of display questions. The teacher asks students *Have you ever been in an accident?*, a referential question. One of the interactions prompted by this question is provided in Scenario E:

Scenario E
S1: China, my mother is a teacher, my father is a teacher. Oh, she go finish, by bicycle, er go to...
S2: House?
S1: No house, go to...
S2: School?
S1: My mother...
T: Mmm
S1 go to her mother.
T: Oh, your grandmother.
Ss: Grandmother.
S1: My grandmother. Oh, yes, by bicycle, by bicycle, oh, is, em, accident. *(Gestures)*
T: In water?
S1: In water, yeah.
T: In a river!
S1: River, yeah, river. Oh, yes, um dead.
Ss: Dead! Dead! Oh! *(General consternation)*

(Adapted from Nunan, 1987, pp. 143-144)

In response to the referential question, Student 1 exhibits increased language use as well as negotiation behaviors. She

150

does not know the English word for "grandmother" but she gets around this lexical roadblock by saying *"My mother...go to her mother,"* in response to which the teacher supplies her with the word. Both the teacher and other students take part in the conversation by helping S1 come up with the words she needs (Ss: *House? School?;* T: *In water?, In a river!*). There is interaction not only between the student and the teacher, but between the student and her classmates. As Nunan states: "The interactions were stimulated principally by the use of referential questions by the teacher on a topic which learners were interested in..." (p. 144). It is important to repeat that Nunan found almost of the teacher's questions to be of the display type (Scenario D), yet when she changed to referential questions as in Scenario E, students became much more participatory.

In an interesting study Brock (1986) found that ESL teachers trained and encouraged to use referential questions ended up asking more referential questions than display (173 vs. 21), as compared to their counterparts who received no training and asked more display than referential questions (114 vs. 24, respectively). But more importantly, Brock's study showed that referential questions prompted students to respond with significantly longer (10 words vs. 4.23 words) and more syntactically complex utterances. The language and behaviors exhibited in Scenario E as well as Brock's study make a compelling argument for the preferred use of referential questions.

COMMUNICATIVE BEHAVIORS AND CONVERSATIONAL GIVE-AND-TAKE

Think about the last time you had a conversation with someone in either your first or second language. What did you talk about? Who raised the subject? How? Did one of you ask a question? Make a comment? Did the other person bring up a new point? Did someone say something that was not clear, prompting the other to ask for clarification?

The effectiveness with which all of us perform the above-mentioned behaviors correlates to how well we communicate with others.

Brooks (e.g., 1993) has found that in language classrooms, it is the teacher who controls conversation topic and topic direction. "...Teachers establish, monitor, and maintain acceptable ways for students to participate in classroom lessons and activities...Since foreign language teachers typically decide who can talk to whom, about what, in what ways, for how long, and in what language, students are usually prevented from engaging each other in any sort of 'real' conversation" (p. 235). As we want our students to be effective speakers of Spanish both inside and outside the classroom, it is important to explore what speaking behaviors should be allowed and encouraged. In other words, what should be the "rules" for class discussions? And what communicative behaviors should we encourage in our students?

In Scenario A on the Halloween discussion, we see two attempts by a student (Jason) to alter the class discussion. After the teacher asks the class what happened last weekend, Jason attempts to change the subject by mentioning tomorrow's quiz. This is an instance of **topic nomination**, as he brings up something not at all related to what the teacher asked (¿Qué pasó este fin de semana?). Although the teacher responds to Jason's point about the quiz, she immediately reverts back to her original question. And after several students in the class mention Halloween, Jason mentions the losing game, an attempt at **topic shift** from Halloween to the game. In both instances (quiz, game), the teacher acknowledges what the student says, yet steers the class discussion in the direction of the topic she wants discussed (Halloween).

Presented below is Scenario F which is similar to Scenario A in that a student is concerned about a quiz, and nominates it as the topic. The teacher requests clarification in response to which the student rephrases the question. At this point the other students in the class try to help **clarify** by repeating the perceived source of the teacher's lack of understanding (i.e., Quiz, quiz).

Again the teacher indicates a lack of understanding. The student then successfully rephrases the question at which point the teacher responds that there will not be a quiz today. As Nunan (1987) indicates, while it is generally the teacher who determines the topic and the order of turns in most situations, student-initiated topic shifts are usually related to either questions of grammar or classroom procedure (the quiz), (p. 139). In addition, the **turn taking** in this exchange does not follow the typical pattern of teacher's turn to speak, then one student's, then teacher's, and so forth; but rather, turn taking is better shared by the students.

Scenario F
S: Quiss?
T: Pardon?
S: It will be quiss? It will be quiss? Quiss?
Ss: Quiz, quiz.
T: Ahmm, sorry? Try again.
S: I ask you....
T: Yes.
S: you give us another quiss?
T: Oh, quiz, oh. No, no, not today, it's not going to be a quiz today, sorry.

(Nunan, 1987, 139)

Scenario G, provided below, initially follows the (I > R > E) pattern with the teacher asking a series of questions about the students' perceptions of the French (*Est-ce que vous avez une impression du caractère français typique, Donna?*). After two students respond with their impressions, the teacher asks a third student, Paul, who seizes the opportunity to modify or shift the topic. In this case, the student converts the focus from making generalizations about the French to making the statement that it is not possible to make generalizations, and the teacher allows him to do so.

Scenario G (This interaction took place in French in a third-quarter French class, but its English translation is provided here. For the original transcription in French, see Appendix B.)

> T: Do you have an impression of the typical French character, Donna?
> S1: They are very romantic.
> T: That's one of the ideas...one of the impressions that people have. Do you have other ideas? Paul?
> S2: The typical Frenchman hates American tourists.
> *(Laughter)*
> T: I think that's true, yes. Do you have other impressions? *(Pause)* Roger, you've just met a French person. What are your impressions?
> S3: Ah...he isn't a typical Frenchman.
> T: He wasn't typical.
> S3: Nobody is typical.
> T: Nobody is typical? In other words it isn't possible to generalize, is that it?
> S3: Yes.
>
> (Guthrie 1984, p. 54)

Both scenarios F and G show conversational give-and-take, with F containing a student-initiated topic nomination, and G a student-initiated topic-shift.

Although the scenarios above feature class interactions involving the teacher, an important issue needs to be addressed concerning **learner-to-learner interaction.** When students are interacting with a partner or in a small group on a communicative activity, what types of communicative behaviors do they exhibit? Several empirical studies (e.g., Doughty and Pica 1986; Porter 1986; Rulon and McCreary 1986) have compared the student language produced during teacher-fronted activities with that produced during paired/group work, and all have found that in the latter individual students had more opportunities to use the language. The studies also suggest that students working in pairs or small groups on communicative activity display a higher number of **negotiation behaviors** such as content clarifications (efforts to clarify what is not understood), confirmation checks (indications that what has been understood has been understood correctly), comprehension checks (efforts to determine that a listener has understood a message), rephrasing, and restating (e.g., Brooks 1992). This has been explained by the suggestion that students feel more comfortable talking with each other and are less inhibited about indicating problems of understanding when talking in pairs or small groups than in front of the class in teacher-centered activity. While engaging in learner-learner interactions, students are also more apt to do **word searches** and to attempt to **"repair"** or improve their language.

A study by Buckwalter (1997) examining the repair behaviors of 58 college students enrolled in first- and second-year Spanish classes engaged in paired communicative activity revealed that the most common repair behavior was self-regulatory. In other words, it was common for individual students to "talk their way" through their own linguistic problems. This is also referred to as "hypothesis testing" in that students experiment with the Spanish words and structures that they have not mastered yet feel need attention within their own developing Spanish systems. The following are examples of individuals students performing self-repairs while engaged in pair activities:

Example A
S: Uh el al-alqui-alquiler es dosciento dólares (p. 109)
Example B
S: Has sido mi compañero de cuatro-cuarto para... (p. 124)
Example C
S: puraja um pur-per es empieza con el pe...pa-pa- uh
   paragua-paraguas (p. 119)
Example D
S: necesitamos limpiar la casa entera por qué nunca a-
   yudarme-ayu-me ayudas con los quehaceres   (p. 110)
                    (Examples adapted from Buckwalter 1997)

Examples A, B, and C show the common self-repair of sounding out words, with the student in Example C going through many steps before coming up with the desired word, *paraguas*. Example D works through a difficulty with syntax, as the speaker initially left out the indirect object pronoun. As Buckwalter states: "pair work encourages self regulation because the learners treated each other as peers and did not interfere with their partners' opportunities to both notice their own difficulties or errors and to rectivy them" (p. 155).

Buckwalter's study revealed that "other repair," namely help provided by a partner, was a far less common behavior. Yet of these other repair behaviors, the most common was one student indicating need for help with a lexical item, and the partner providing it. Examples of other repair for vocabulary are presented in E and F:

Example E
S1:   haga una cita para uh para el lunes de la semana…
S2:   próximo?
S1:   Sí gracias.   (p. 94)

Example F
S1:   Tuve una fiesta uh esta noche? No
S2:   ¿Anoche?
S1:   Anoche sí y um alguien… (p. 130)
                    (Examples adapted from Buckwalter 1997)

Returning to the questions posed at the beginning of this section, in most conversations, all participants share the responsibility and have opportunities to either begin or alter the topic of conversation. One of the goals of the communicative Spanish classroom is to teach students not only how to hear and comprehend the language, but also how to successfully participate in conversations. Providing that students are respectful of others, they should be encouraged to participate in behaviors such as topic nomination, topic shift, active sharing of turns, negotiation of meaning (e.g., asking for clarification), and repair. Studies on learner-to-learner interaction of students engaged in communicative activity suggest that increased language use as well as greater instances of communicative behaviors are displayed during meaning-based paired and small-group activity. When students are involved in communicative activities, whether teacher-fronted or student-centered, they should be encouraged to develop the communicative, negotiative, and conversational give-and-take behaviors associated with real-life communication.

ACTIVITY PURPOSE AND TEACHER BELIEFS

Upon examination of different classroom interactions, a mismatch in perception is often detected between what teachers perceive to be the purpose of an activity, and what the outcome of the activity actually is.

As one point of reference, let's examine the following classroom exchange between a Spanish teacher and a second-year student reported in Brooks (1993):

Teacher: ¿Cuántos años tiene tu papá, Antonio?
Anthony: 37 años.
Teacher: Uh huh. Mi padreeeeee....
Anthony: Mi padre tiene 37 años.
Teacher: Bien. Mi padre tiene 37 años. Muy bien, Antonio.

(p. 234)

At first glance it appears from the teacher's question that she is interested in learning the age of Anthony's father. Yet from her response to Anthony's answer (T: *Uh huh. Mi padreeeeee...*), it becomes clear that what is most important is that the student answer in a complete sentence. In fact, this is so important to the teacher that in addition to rewarding Anthony for answering in a complete sentence (T: *Bien*), she repeats Anthony's complete sentence herself (T: *Mi padre tiene 37 años*). As the rest of the students witness this exchange, they quickly learn that they are expected to answer all questions in complete sentences, including questions that in "real-life" do not require complete-sentence responses. Whereas the teacher believes that it is important to train her students to answer in complete sentences, her students learn that *how* they answer (i.e., in a complete sentence), may be more important than *what* they say. Students may also get the mistaken impression that people who speak Spanish in real life always speak in complete sentences. Yet as in real life where communication and information exchange take precedence, short-answer questions (*e.g., ¿Cómo estás?, ¿Adónde vas?*), deserve short answers. If the teacher wants students to produce longer discourse, he or she should ask open-ended questions as well as provide students with meaning-focused opportunities to do so.

One of the reasons that many teachers have their students carry out pair and small-group work is because they wish to provide their students more opportunities to communicate. Yet research has shown that if students believe that the focus of the activity is on the practice of forms, they will turn most of their attention to the form-driven aspects of the practice and little attention to the communication (Brooks 1990; Kinginger 1990). If the teacher spends a lot of time drilling students on particular lexical or grammatical features, students when working in pairs or groups will do the same. Look at the following interaction of pair work from Brooks (1990):

S1:   ¿Cómo son Alberto y Antonio?
S2:   Alberto y Antonio son buenos
S1:   Muy bien. ¿Cómo es Luisa?
S2:   Luisa ahhh es Luisa. lindas   lindas
S1:   Lindas o linda
S2:   Linda. You're right.
S1:   Muy bien. It's not plural. OK.
(Adapted from Brooks 1990, pp. 158-159)

As mentioned earlier in this chapter, the teacher's focus prior to this exchange had been on the use of correct adjective endings. By having students work together in pairs, the teacher expected students to be expressive and to describe the pictures provided them. Instead, students imitated the teacher's behaviors (i.e., one student "plays teacher" and asks a question, the student answers it in a complete sentence, the "teacher" corrects grammar and rewards the student for answering correctly). Brooks found that students display the same corrective and conversational behaviors modeled by their instructor. On the flip side, if teachers model communicative behaviors, their students are more likely to do the same.

Another example of form-focused teacher discourse behaviors comes from a study conducted by Hall (1995) from a Spanish 1 classroom:

Scenario H

Teacher:	*(begins by playing a tape of songs by Gloria Estefan)* Es música, ¿no?
	Música, ¿no?
Julio	no
Teacher:	Es música. Es música. Es música. Ahora señor, ¿te gusta? ¿te gusta la música?
Julio:	No me gusta.
Teacher:	No me gusta
Julio:	No me gusta
Teacher:	No me gusta la música. ¿Te gusta la música? No me gusta la música.
	¿Te gusta la música?
Ss:	I do sí sí yeah sí
Rafael:	Aw man where you goin'
Teacher:	Sí, me gusta la música. ¿Te gusta la música?
Andrea:	Sí.

(Hall 1995, p. 44)

After the teacher plays a tape of music, asks and repeats a question (*Es música, ¿no?*; *¿Te gusta? ¿Te gusta la música?*), then asks another question, it appears that he is establishing music—or some aspect of music—to be the topic of interaction. (If he had wanted to develop this topic, the teacher and class could first find out whether his students liked these or other Gloria Estefan songs, procede to find out what musical artists or groups the students like, then explore what their favorite kinds of music are, and so forth.) Instead, the teacher engages in what Hall calls "lexical chaining," referred to as "linking lexical items through the repetition of all or part of the previous utterance" (p. 44). The teacher makes an utterance, repeats all or part of it, and then may add a related word to the "interaction." In this example the teacher asks Julio *¿Te gusta la música?,* to which Julio responds *No me gusta* which the teacher repeats, and then Julio repeats, and then the teacher adds another word: *No me gusta la música. ¿Te gusta la música?* Hall found in observations of this class that throughout the semester, the I > R > E pattern with lexical chaining—resulting in the practice of particular lexicon and structures (e.g., *te gusta/me gusta*), was the primary feature of this teacher's interactional talk. The result of this was that early on in the semester, students realized that the purpose of the teacher's language was to get them to "practice" using simple strings of words used in simple ways. On several occasions at the beginning of the term, students thought that the teacher was opening topics for discussions and wanted to know their opinions. Yet after each of these attempts by students, the teacher returned to the practice of lexical chaining. The message that students received was that interacting in Spanish consists of answering the teacher's question using the words that he uses (T: *¿Te gusta la música?* S: *Sí, me gusta la música*), but it does not consist of expression their opinions and talking about real topics. As Hall indicates: "...learning to competently participate in an interactive practice occurs more readily when the learners know what is going on i.e., the purpose of the interaction, including what count as relevant topics and rhetorical structures, and when the talk is oriented to them. Unfortunately, little of this kind of learning potential is available to the students in the practice examined here...Furthermore, since they never really move beyond the activity of lexical chaining, the learning potential embedded in what they *are* exposed to is quite limited and limiting" (p. 55).

There is a "mismatch" here between the teacher's use of language and his intent. The teacher believes that he is providing his students with a rich linguistic experience because he uses the target language almost exclusively, and he expects students to speak in Spanish. What he doesn't realize is that he is not providing his students with the interactive environments surrounding actual topics or themes that lead to greater and richer language use.

Scenario I presented below is intended as a point of comparison with Scenario H. This exchange occurred in an ESL class of 10-year-old native French speakers, reported in Lightbown and Spada (1993). Prior to the exchange, the teacher asked the students to write down things that "bug" them.

Scenario I

S1: It bugs me when a bee string me.

T: Oh, when a bee stings me.

S1: Stings me.

T: Do you get stung often? Does that happen often? The bee stinging many times?

S1: Yeah.

T: Often? *(Teacher addresses and resolves a management problem.)*

S2: It bugs me *(inaudible)* and my sister put on my clothes.

T: Ah! She--borrows your clothes? When you're older, you may appreciate it because you can switch clothes, maybe. *(Teacher checks another student's written work.)*

S3: It bugs me when I'm sick and my brother doesn't help me--my--my brother, 'cause he--me--

T: OK. You know--when *(inaudible)* sick, you're sick at home in bed and you say, oh, to your brother or your sister: "Would you please get me a drink of water?" "Ah! Drop dead!" you know, "Go play in the traffic!" You know, it's not very nice. Martin!

.... (Adapted from Lightbown and Spada, p. 76)

In contrast to Scenario H, the primary focus of the interaction in Scenario G is on the exchange of meaning surrounding a particular topic. The students know what the topic is, and everything said relates to that topic. The teacher listens to what students say and asks related questions to elicit more information from them, and she expands on what they say. The teacher corrects students only when she feels it is necessary (S: *A bee string me;* T: *A bee stings me*). Throughout the interaction the teacher and her students stick to what "bugs" the students, the specified topic.

In this section we have raised the issue of "mismatch" between what teachers may perceive to be the purpose of an activity, and what the outcome of the activity actually is. Teachers who insist their students answer in complete sentences in response to questions that do not require complete sentence answers, as well as those who respond more to form than to content, may inadvertently convey the message to students that *how* they say something is more important to *what* they say. A logical reaction to this on the part of most students could be: *I have to say everything correctly, so I'd better be careful and say as little as possible!* Similarly, research suggests that students whose teachers emphasize form-focused instruction will display these same behaviors when they are engaged in pair work on "supposedly" communicative activities. We have also seen an example of teacher language which consists of lexical chaining, or the combining of certain words and expressions. Students are then asked to respond using the same lexical chain. This type of interaction does not provide students the opportunity to develop their Spanish around meaningful topics, something that can be done in the classroom (as in Scenario I), and which is done regularly in real-life interaction outside the classroom.

SUMMARY

This chapter on Classroom Interaction begins with a quote from the *Standards* that stresses the importance of providing students with opportunities to use the target language (Spanish) to communicate in a wide range of activities. This chapter set out to illustrate common classroom interaction practices, with an eye on highlighting those that provide better opportunities for our students to develop their language proficiency.

Before describing common classroom practices, however, a brief description of caregiver talk, foreigner talk, and teacher talk was provided. What we see there is the disconnect between what happens in real life (with caregiver and foreigner talk), and what happens in the classroom (teacher talk). Teacher talk tends to follow the I (Interaction) > R (Response) > E (Evaluation/Feedback) pattern, with the teacher doing all the initiating and all the evaluating, with the evaluation tending to focus on grammatical accuracy, not on the message. To encourage greater student participation, language teachers are reminded that caregivers and those interacting with non-native speakers are much more likely to attend to *what* a person has to say than to *how* he or she says it.

In the section on Class Discussions, examples of classroom transcripts from open-ended discussion questions and task-based activity are compared. Although open-ended discussions may arise spontaneously, we nonetheless recommend that task-based activity design be implemented as it will garner greater student participation. Another reason to use task-based activities is to enhance classroom management.

We also discuss question types, comparing and contrasting display and referential questions. Research suggests that the use of referential questions promotes longer and more complex student responses.

The "Communicative Behaviors and Conversational Give-and-Take" section advocates classroom interaction practices that encourage students to display the behaviors that will make them successful conversationalists, both inside and outside the classroom. These behaviors include topic nomination, topic shift, and active turn taking. Research on learner-to-learner interaction suggests that when working in pairs or small groups on communicative activities, students have more opportunities to use language, and to engage in negotiating behaviors that help them "talk their way" through their self-identified language difficulties.

In "Activity Purpose and Teacher Beliefs" we try to illuminate the differences between what teachers wish to achieve in a given interaction activity, and what they may actually achieve. For example, teachers who ask short-answer questions yet insist their students answer in complete sentences may give students the impression that form is more important than message; and as a result, this will likely encourage students to be so concerned with form that they not express themselves more freely and openly. By the same token, teachers who tend to lead question-and-answer sessions in which drills are practiced, will find these same behaviors imitated by students when they work in pairs or small groups. Another interaction behavior focussed on the practice of asking questions using simple strings of words. These strings of words did not relate to any real themes or topics. Not structuring lessons and classroom interactions around real topics does not provide students the opportunity to develop the extended, theme-related language they need to better function in Spanish.

Returning to chapter-opening Question 1, two sample classroom interactions are provided. In the first (Example A) in which the teacher asks a student ¿Cómo te llamas?, and after the student gives his name in an incomplete sentence, the teacher responds in a real-life manner by saying Mucho gusto. The second, Example, B, sees the teacher asking the same question but when the student gives his name in an incomplete sentence, recasts his answer in a complete sentence T: Me llamo Nick. The student then repeats after the teacher, and the teacher rewards him (Muy bien) for answering in a complete sentence. Although it could be argued that both teachers in Examples A and B are a)...interested in learning the student's name, it seems less true for the teacher in Example B because what the teacher responds to is the incomplete sentence. Because of this, we can say that of course Example B shows that b) The teacher expects students to answer in complete sentences, and c) What the student says is less important than how he says it. The teacher in Example B e)...rewards the student for correctly answering. The teacher in Example A clearly indicates interest in learning the student's name ("a"), and also indicates that d) What the student says is more important than how he says it, and the teacher f) ...responds to the student in a "real-life" manner.

In reference to Question 2, in this chapter we have attempted to show that How teachers structure and use Spanish in the classroom...a) informs students what behaviors the teacher considers acceptable, b) affects the way students use Spanish, and c) suggests to students how Spanish is used outside the classroom, in other words, d) All of the above. And it is of course up to us to create classroom environments that privilege students' successful development of interpersonal communication.

As we begin the chapter with one quote, we end it with another:

"In order to learn to communicate, learners must be engaged in communicating throughout the developmental process. ...Foreign language research on 'communicative tasks' demonstrates (for example, Brooks 1990; Kinginger 1990 [cited in Chapter 5]), learners use their instructors and their past learning experiences as models. If their instructors are overly concerned with grammar and pieces of language, or give mixed messages about what is important during a given activity, learners will abandon true communication during such activities. If instructors themselves use language meaningfully and are constantly attempting to communicate with learners, then the learners in turn will attempt to communicate with each other when tasks with clear information goals are set up for them. In short, the acquisition of communicative language ability must begin with the instructor using language to interpret, express, and negotiate some kind of meaning with students."

(VanPatten 1991, p. 70)

APPENDIX A

Lesson Plans for the Experimental Groups: Discussion
Questions and Task-Based Activity (Lee 2000, pp. 46-74;
Original Spanish provided by author-researcher)

Discussion Questions
Phase 1. Asociaciones
    ¿Qué asocian Uds. con el término *bilingüe*?
    ¿Qué asocian Uds. con el término *bicultural*?
Phase 2. Llegando a ser bilingüe/bicultural
    ¿Cómo se llega a ser bilingüe?
    ¿Cómo se llega a ser bicultural?
Phase 3. Conclusiones
    ¿Se llega a ser bilingüe y bicultural de la misma manera?
    ¿Son dos procesos diferentes?
    ¿Se puede ser bilingüe sin ser bicultural?
    ¿Es posible apreciar otra cultura sin saber su lengua?

Task-Based Activity
Phase 1. Asociaciones
Paso 1. En grupos de cuatro, preparen una lista de todo lo que
asocian con los términos bilingüe y bicultural.
    Bilingüe   Bicultural
    1. _____   1. _____
    2. _____   2. _____
    3. _____   3. _____
    4. _____   4. _____
    5. _____   5. _____

Phase 2. Llegando a ser bilingüe/bicultural
Paso 2. En sus grupos, comenten la pregunta: ¿Cómo pueden
Uds. llegar a ser bilingües? Propongan varias ideas.
1._____
2._____
3._____
4._____

¿Otras ideas?

Paso 3. Ahora, en grupos, comenten la pregunta, ¿Cómo pueden Uds. llegar a ser biculturales? Propongan varias ideas.

1._____

2._____

3._____

4._____

Phase 3. Conclusiones

Paso 4. ¿Qué te parece? ¿Se llega a ser bilingüe y bicultural de la misma manera? ¿Son dos procesos diferentes? ¿Se puede ser bicultural sin ser bilingüe? ¿Se puede ser bilingüe sin ser bicultural? ¿Es posible apreciar otra cultura sin saber su lengua?

APPENDIX B

This is the original transcript from the third-quarter French class.

T: Est-ce que vous avez une impression du caractère français typique, Donna?

S1: Ils sont très romantiques.

T: C'est une des idées…une des impressions qu'on a. Est-ce que vous avez d'autres idées? Paul?

S2: Le Français typique déteste les tourists américains.
    (Laughter)

T: Je pense que c'est vrai, oui. Vous avez d'autres impressions? *(Pause)* Roger, vous venez de faire la connaissance d'un Française. Quelles sont vos impressions?

S3: Ah…c'est…c'est ne Français typique.

T: Il n'était pas typique.

S3: Ne personne est typique.

T: Personne n'est typique. C'est à dire qu'eil n'est pas possible de généraliser, c'est ça?

S3: Oui.

    …   (Guthrie 1984, pp. 48-49)

APPLICATION ACTIVITIES FOR REFLECTION AND DISCUSSION

1. Read over the following snippets of conversation. Which represent caregiver talk, foreigner talk, and teacher talk? Give reasons for why you identified each as you did.

    a. X: I love you to pieces.

    Y: I love you three pieces.

    (Adapted from Lightbown and Spada 1993, p. 6)

    b. (E = Erika)

    X: Erika, ¿Te gustan las zanahorias?

    E: Sí.

    X: ¿Qué vegetal serías tú?

    E: No sé.

    X: ¿No sabes?

    E: No sabes.

    X: No sé.

    E: Yo no pienso sobre qué vegetal sería.

    (Adapted from unpublished data collected by Liskin-Gasparro 1998)

    c. (D = Doug)

    X: Doug, you have dream after your life?

    D: Whaddya mean?

    X: OK. Everybody have some dream. What doing—Whatyou want--after your life, you have it?

    D: You mean after I die?

    X: No no. I mean next couple years or long time. OK. Before I have big dream. I move to States, now I have it. This kind you have it?

    D: Security, I suppose. Not necessarily financial, although that looms large at the present time.

    (Schmidt 1983, p. 165, cited in Nunan 1992)

    d. X: I putted the plates on the table!

    Y: You mean, I **put** the plates on the table.

    X: No, **I** putted them on all by myself.

    (Adapted from Lightbown and Spada 1993, p. 14)

    e. X: ¿Tú lavas la ropa?

    Y: Ahhh me lavo

X: Sí

Y: Me lavo

X: ¿Tú lavas la ropa? No a ti misma, la ropa. **Yo...**

Y: Yo lavo la ropa

X: Con pronombre directo

Y: Yo la lavo.

X: Muy bien.

(Adapted from unpublished data collected by Liskin-Gasparro 1998)

2. In this chapter you saw examples of conversations that included caregiver talk and foreigner talk.

   a. Try to observe the interactions of a caregiver interacting with a small child, and a native speaker (of English or Spanish) interacting with a non-native speaker of the language. Which of the following adjustments are made by the caregiver and the native speaker?:

   _____ slowing of speech

   _____ intonation used to stress or clarify

   _____ rephrasing

   _____ repetition of key words

   _____ error correction

   _____ response to message (and/or to form)

   other?:

   b. What are the similarities and differences between the caregiver talk and foreigner talk interactions you observed? What are the positive features of these interactions that should be adopted in the Spanish classroom?

3. Do some "action" research in your Spanish class. First, conduct an open-ended class discussion on an academic topic (*¿La asistencia a clase debe ser obligatoria o no?*). On another day, design a task-based lesson on a comparable academic topic and after students have worked on a task, lead them in a report-back or follow-up discussion. Audio record each of these sessions, and analyze each transcription for the following:

a. How many students participate in the discussion vs. task-based follow-up formats?

b. How much information is shared in each format?

c. Does the format influence whether students nominate or change topics?

d. In which format is the class more participatory?

e. In which format are students better behaved?

4. Record yourself leading your class in an information exchange (i.e., meaning focused) questions and answers activity. Analyze your behaviors by answering the following questions:

a. Do I ask more display or more referential questions?

b. Do I insist that students answer in complete sentences (when a complete-sentence answer is not necessary in "real-life" Spanish)?

c. Do I respond to my students' message (i.e., I ask related follow-up questions) or do I respond more to form (i.e., I correct their grammar)?

5. Once you have had a chance to record and analyze the way you use Spanish in your class, identify what you really like about your language use and then identify what you would like to work on. (It is recommended that you record yourself again every few weeks to check on your progress!)

6. Research on the language and behaviors exhibited by students working in pairs or small groups on communicative activities provides support for this student-centered pedagogical practice. In order to examine your students' learner-learner interaction, you may want to occasionally record one or two small groups of students. (Our experience is that most students do not mind having their group work recorded.) Do individual students produce longer utterances than they do in teacher-fronted activity? What negotiation behaviors (e.g., content clarification, confirmation checks, comprehension checks) do they exhibit? Do they engage in self-regulatory behaviors (e.g., "sounding out")? Do students help one another? In what ways?

WORKS CITED

American Council on the Teaching of Foreign Languages. 2001.
Oral Proficiency Testing and the ACTFL Proficiency Guidelines.
Retrieved August 5, 2001 from http://www.actfl.org.

Asher, James. 1977. *Learning Another Language Through Actions:
The Complete Teacher's Guide*. Los Gatos, CA: Sky Oaks
Publications.

Ballman, Terry. 1996. Integrating Vocabulary, Grammar, and Culture:
A Model Five-Day Communicative Lesson Plan. *Foreign Language
Annals* 29: 37-44.

——. 1997. Enhancing Beginning Language Courses Through
Content-Enriched Instruction. *Foreign Language Annals* 30: 173-
186.

——. 1998. From Teacher-Centered to Learner-Centered: Guidelines
for Sequencing and Presenting the Elements of a Foreign Language
Class. In *The Coming of Age of the Profession: Issues and
Emerging Ideas for the Teaching of Foreign Languages,* edited by
Jane Harper, Madeleine Lively, and Mary Williams, 97-111.
Boston: Heinle & Heinle.

——. 2000. Sample AP Spanish Language Course Description and
Syllabus. Retrieved May 30, 2001 from
http://www.collegeboard.org/ap/spanish/sample_syllabus/index.html.
New York: College Entrance Examination Board.

Bearden, Rebecca. 2001. An Interactionist Study of Small-Group Oral
Discussion vs. Computer-Assisted Class Discussion between Native
Speakers and Nonnative Learners of Spanish. Paper presented at the
conference of the American Association for Applied Linguistics, St.
Louis, MO.

Birckbirchler, Diane W., and Kathryn A. Corl. 1993. Perspectives on Proficiency: Teachers, Students, and the Materials that They Use. In *Reflecting on Proficiency from a Classroom Perspective*, edited by June K. Phillips, pp. 115-158. Northeast Conference Reports. Lincolnwood, IL: National Textbook Company.

Brock, Cynthia A. 1986. The Effects of Referential Questions on ESL Classroom Discourse. *TESOL Quarterly* 20: 47-59.

Brooks, Frank B. 1990. Foreign Language Learning: A Social Interaction Perspective. In *Second Language Acquisition-ForeignLanguage Learning: Perspectives on Research and Practice,* edited by Bill VanPatten and James F. Lee, 153-169. Clevedon, UK: Multilingual Matters.

———. 1992. Spanish III Learners Talking to One another Through a Jigsaw Task. *Canadian Modern Language Review* 48: 696-717.

———. 1993. Some Problems and Caveats in 'Communicative' Discourse: Toward a Conceptualization of the Foreign Language Classroom. *Foreign Language Annals* 26: 233-242.

Buckwalter, Peggy A. 1997. Repair in Classroom Dyadic Talk-in-Interaction: An Exploration of an Approach to the Analysis of L2 Learner-Learner Discourse. Ph.D. diss., University of Texas at Austin.

Canale, Michael, and Merrill Swain. 1980. Theoretical Bases of Communicative Approaches to Second Language Teaching and Testing. *Applied Linguistics* 1: 1-47.

Center for Advanced Research on Language Acquisition. 2001. Contextualized speaking assessment, University of Minnesota Language Assessment Project. Retrieved August 5, 2001 from http://carla.acad.umn.edu/CoSA.html.

Center for Applied Linguistics. 2000. Foreign Language NAEP National Consensus Building Project. Retrieved July 13, 2001 from http://www.cal.org/flnaep/.

———. 2001. Simulated oral proficiency interviews. Retrieved August 5, 2001 from http://www.cal.org/tests/fltests.html.

Chaudron, Craig. 1988. *Second Language Classrooms*. Cambridge: Cambridge University Press.

Cohen, Andrew. 1994. *Assessing Language Ability in the Classroom*. 2nd ed. Boston: Heinle and Heinle.

College Entrance Examination Board. AP Spanish. 2000 Free-Response Questions. Retrieved July 13, 2001 from http://www.collegeboard.org/ap/students/spanish/frq00/index.html.

Corder, S. P. 1967. The Significance of Learners' Errors. *IRAL* 5: 161-169.

Donato, Richard. 1994. Collective Scaffolding in Language Learning. In *Vygotskian Approaches to Second Language Research*, edited by James P. Lantolf and Gabriela Appel, pp. 33-56. Norwood, NJ: Ablex.

Dörnyei, Zoltan. 1994. Motivation and Motivating in the Foreign Language Classroom. *Modern Language Journal* 78: 273-284.

Doughty, Catherine, and Jessica Williams. 1998. *Focus on Form in Classroom Second Language Acquisition*. Cambridge: Cambridge University Press.

Doughty, Catherine, and Teresa Pica. 1986. Information Gap Tasks: Do They Facilitate Acquisition? *TESOL Quarterly* 20: 305-326.

Ellis, Rod. 1986. *Understanding Second Language Acquisition*. Oxford: Oxford University Press.

———. 1994. *The Study of Second Language Acquisition*. Oxford: Oxford University Press.

Finkel, Donald L., and G. Stephen Monk. 1983. Teachers and Learning Groups: Dissolution of the Atlas Complex. In *Learning in Groups*, edited by Clark Bouton and Russell Y. Garth, 83-97. San Francisco: Jossey-Bass, as cited in Lee and VanPatten 1995.

Gardner, Robert C., and Wallace E. Lambert. 1972. *Attitudes and Motivation in Second Language Learning*. Rowley, MA: Newbury House.

Gass, Susan M., and Evangeline Marlos Varonis. 1994 . Input, Interaction, and Second Language Production. *Studies in Second Language Acquisition* 16: 283-302.

Guntermann, Gail, ed. 2000. *Teaching Spanish with the Five C's: A Blueprint for Success*, Volume II of the AATSP Professional Development Series Handbook for Teachers K-16. Fort Worth, TX: Harcourt College Publishers.

Guthrie, Elizabeth M. Leemann. 1984. Intake, Communication, and Second-Language Teaching. In *Initiatives in Communicative Language Teaching*, edited by Sandra J. Savignon and Margie S. Berns, 35-54. Reading, MA: Addison-Wesley.

Hadley, Alice Omaggio. 2000. *Teaching Language in Context*. 3rd. Boston: Heinle & Heinle.

Hall, Joan K. 1995. "Aw, man, where you goin'?": Classroom Interaction and the Development of L2 Interactional Competence. *Issues in Applied Linguistics* 6: 37-62.

Harlow, Linda L., and Judith A. Muyskens. 1994 . Priorities for Intermediate Language Instruction. *Modern Language Journal* 78: 141-154.

Harper, Jane, and Madeleine Lively. 1991. *HOTStuff for Teachers of Spanish*. Arlington, TX: Harper and Lively Educational Services.

Hatch, Evelyn. 1978. Discourse Analysis and Second Language Acquisition. In *Second Language Acquisition: A Book of Readings*, edited by Evelyn Hatch, 401-435. Rowley, MA: Newbury House.

Hymes, Dell. 1971. *On Communicative Competence*. Philadelphia: University of Pennsylvania Press.

Kinginger, Celeste. 1990. *Task Variation and Classroom Learner Discourse*. Ph.D. diss., University of Illinois Urbana-Champaign.

Krashen, Stephen D. 1982 . *Principles and Practice in Second Language Acquisition*. New York: Pergamon Press.

———. 1985. The Input Hypothesis: Issues and Implications. New York: Longman.

Krashen, Stephen D., and Tracy D. Terrell. 1983. *The Natural Approach: Language Acquisition in the Classroom*. Hayward, CA: Alemany.

Lambert, Wallace E. 1974. Culture and Language as Factors in Learning and Education. In *Cultural Factors in Learning and Education*, edited by F. Aboud and R. Meade. Bellingham, WA: 5th Western Washington Symposium on Learning.

Larsen-Freeman, Diane, and Michael H. Long. 1991. *An Introduction* to Second Language Acquisition. New York: Longman.

Lee, James F. 1995. Using Task-Based Activities to Restructure Class Discussions. *Foreign Language Annals* 28: 437-446.

———. 2000. Tasks and Communicating in Language Classrooms. New York: McGraw-Hill.

———. June 5, 2001. Personal communication about the study reported in Lee 2000.

Lee, James F., and Albert Valdman, eds. 2000. *Form and Meaning: Multiple Perspectives*. AAUSC Issues in Language Program Direction. Boston: Heinle and Heinle.

Lee, James F., and Bill VanPatten. 1995. *Making Communicative Language Teaching Happen*. New York: McGraw-Hill.

Lightbown, Patsy. M., and Nina Spada. 1993. *How Languages Are Learned*. Oxford: Oxford University Press.

Liskin-Gasparro, Judith E. 1988. Unpublished pedagogical materials, Middlebury College.

———. 1993. Talking About the Past: An Analysis of the Discourse of Intermediate High and Advanced Level Speakers of Spanish. Ph.D. diss., University of Texas at Austin.

———. 1995. Unpublished raw data, University of Iowa.

———. 1996. Assessment: From Content Standards to Student Performance. In *National Standards: A Catalyst for Reform*, edited by Robert C. Layafette, pp. 169-196. Lincolnwood, IL: National Textbook Company.

———. 1998. Unpublished raw data, University of Iowa.

———. 1999. Tips for Managing Pair and Small-Group Activities. Unpublished pedagogical materials, University of Iowa.

———. 2001a. Reviewing the Reviews: A Modest History of Policy and Practices. *Modern Language Journal* 85: 77-91.

———. 2001b. Unpublished pedagogical materials, University of Iowa.

Long, Michael H. 1983. Native Speaker/Non Native Speaker Conversation and the Negotiation of Comprehensible Input. *Applied Linguistics* 4: 126-141.

Long, Michael H., and Patricia A. Porter. 1985. Group Work, Interlanguage Talk, and Second Language Acquisition. *TESOL Quarterly* 19: 207-228.

Long, Michael H., and Charlene Sato. 1983. Classroom Foreigner Talk Discourse: Forms and Functions of Teachers' Questions. In *Classroom Oriented Research in Second Language Acquisition*, edited by Harold Seliger and Michael H. Long, 268-286. Rowley, MA: Newbury House.

Marinelli, Patti J., and Lizette Mujica Laughlin. 1998. *Puentes*. 2nd ed. Boston: Heinle & Heinle.

Mehan, Hugh. 1979. *Learning Lessons: Social Organization in the Classroom.* Cambridge, MA: Harvard University Press.

National Council of State Supervisors of Foreign Languages. 2000. State Reports. Retrieved July 13, 2001 from http://www.ncssfl.org/state.htm.

National Standards in Foreign Language Education Project. 1996. *Standards for Foreign Language Learning: Preparing for the 21st Century.* Lawrence, KS: Allen Press.

———. 1999. Lawrence, KS: Allen Press.

New Jersey World Languages Curriculum Framework. 1999. Trenton, NJ: New Jersey Department of Education.

Nunan, David. 1987. Communicative Language Teaching: Making It Work. *English Language Teaching Journal* 41: 136-145.

Perrett, Gillian. 1990. The Language Testing Interview: A Reappraisal. In *Individualizing the Assessment of Language Abilities*, edited by John H. A. L. de Jong and Douglas K. Stevenson, 225-238. Clevedon, England: Multilingual Matters.

Phillips, June K., and Robert M. Terry. 1999. *Foreign Language Standards: Linking Research, Theories, and Practices.* Chicago, IL: National Textbook Company.

Porter, Patricia A. 1986. How Learners Talk to Each Other: Input and Interaction in Task-Centered Discussion. In *Talking to Learn: Conversation in Second Language Acquisition,* edited by Richard R. Day, 200-224. Rowley, MA: Newbury House.

Reddy, Michael J. 1979. The Conduit Metaphor—A Case of Frame Conflict in Our Language About Language. In *Metaphor and Thought*, edited by Andrew Ortuny, 285-324. Cambridge: Cambridge University Press.

Renjilian-Burgy, Joy, Ana Beatriz Chiquito, and Susan M. Mraz. 1999. Caminos Activities Manual. Boston: Houghton Mifflin.

Richards, Jack C., and Theodore S. Rodgers. 1986. *Approaches and Methods in Language Teaching*. Cambridge: Cambridge University Press.

Rulon, Kathryn A., and Jan McCreary. 1986. Negotiation of Content: Teacher-Fronted and Small-Group Interaction. In *Talking to Learn: Conversation in Second Language Acquisition,* edited by Richard R. Day, 182-199. Rowley, MA: Newbury House.

Savignon, Sandra J. 1972. *Communicative Competence: An Experiment in Foreign Language Teaching*. Philadelphia: Center or Curriculum Development.

———. 1997. Communicative Competence: Theory and Practice. 2d ed. New York: McGraw-Hill.

Schwartz, Bonnie. 1993. On Explicit and Negative Data Effecting and Affecting Competence and Linguistic Behavior. *Studies in Second Language Acquisition* 15: 147-163.

Shrum, Judith L., and Eileen W. Glisan. 2000. Chapter 3: Organizing Content and Planning for Integrated Language Instruction. *Teacher's Handbook: Contextualized Language Instruction*, 48-74. 2nd ed. Boston: Heinle & Heinle.

Sinclair, John McHardy, and R. Malcolm Coulthard. 1975. *Towards An Analysis of Discourse: The English Used by Teachers and Pupils*. Oxford: Oxford University Press.

Standards for Foreign Language Learning in the 21st Century. 1999. Lawrence, KS: Allen Press, Inc.

Standards for Foreign Language Learning: Preparing for the 21st Century. 1996. Yonkers, NY: National Standards in Foreign Language Education Project.

Swain, Merrill. 1985. Communicative Competence: Some Roles for Comprehensible Input and Comprehensible Output in its Development. In *Input in Second Language Acquisition*, edited by Susan M. Gass and Carol Madden, 235-253. Cambridge, MA: Newbury House, 235-53.

Terrell, Tracy D. 1986. Acquisition in the Natural Approach: The Binding/Access Framework. *Modern Language Journal* 70: 213-227.

Valette, Rebecca M. 1991. Proficiency and the Prevention of Fossilization—An Editorial. *Modern Language Journal* 75: 325-328.

VanPatten, Bill. 1987. Classroom Learners' Acquisition of *Ser* and *Estar:* Accounting for Developmental Patterns. In *Foreign Language Learning: A Research Perspective*, edited by Bill VanPatten, Trisha R. Dvorak, and James F. Lee, 61-75. Rowley, MA: Newbury House.

——. 1988. How Juries Get Hung: Problems with the Evidence for a Focus on Form. *Language Learning* 38: 243-260.

——. 1991. The Foreign Language Classroom as a Place to Communicate. In *Foreign Language Acquisition Research and the Classroom*, edited by Barbara F. Freed, 54-73. Boston, MA: D. C. Heath.

——. 1993. Grammar Teaching for the Acquisition-Rich Classroom. Foreign Language Annals 26: 435-450.

——. 1996. Input Processing and Grammar Instruction: Theory and Research. Norwood, NJ: Ablex.

Young, Richard, and Michael Milanovic. 1992. Discourse Variation in Oral Proficiency Interviews. *Studies in Second Language Acquisition* 14: 403-424.

ABOUT THE AUTHORS

Terry L. Ballman is Associate Professor of Spanish and Head of the Department of Modern Foreign Languages at Western Carolina University. In addition to coordinating lower-division language programs and supervising student teachers, Professor Ballman has taught Spanish language and linguistics courses, as well as methods courses for foreign language, ESL, and bilingual teachers. She is a recipient of several teaching awards, including one from the University of Texas where she received her Ph.D. She is a member of the Team of Professional Development Workshops sponsored by AATSP and the Office of Education of the Embassy of Spain. A coauthor of two Spanish textbooks, Professor Ballman has published articles in research volumes and journals, including in the area of lesson planning. You are welcome to contact her at tballman@email.wcu.edu.

Judith E. Liskin-Gasparro is Associate Professor of Spanish and Director of the General Education Program in the Department of Spanish and Portuguese at the University of Iowa. She is also the co-director of FLARE (Foreign Language Acquisition Research and Education), an interdisciplinary unit at the University of Iowa that operates a doctoral program in second language acquisition. She currently serves as the Associate Editor for Reviews of the *Modern Language Journal*. Professor Liskin-Gasparro teaches courses in teaching methods and applied linguistics; her interest in the relationships between second language acquisition and language teaching has informed her recent research on the effectiveness of various techniques of error correction and on students' awareness of their own linguistic development during an immersion experience. Professor Liskin-Gasparro has written extensively on assessment issues, particularly oral proficiency testing, and has done research on oral narratives by learners of Spanish. Her email address is judith-liskin-gasparro@uiowa.edu.

180

Paul B. Mandell is Assistant Professor of Spanish Applied Linguistics and Second Language Acquisition in the Department of Modern and Classical Languages at the University of Houston where he is also the Director of the Spanish Basic Language Program. He received his Ph.D. from the University of Illinois at Urbana-Champaign and has taught Spanish at the high school, community college, and university levels. Professor Mandell currently teaches graduate and undergraduate courses in Spanish linguistics and teaching methods. His current research interests include how second language (L2) learners' knowledge of syntax develops over time. He has published articles on verb movement in Spanish and the reliability of L2 learner grammaticality judgment test data. He can be reached at pmandell@uh.edu.

Questions or comments? Please contact the authors at their email addresses listed above.